COME ALIVE

by
Mother Mary Francis, P.C.C.

Franciscan Herald Press • 1434 West 51st Street
Chicago, Illinois
60609

COME ALIVE by Mother Mary Francis, P.C.C. Copyright © 1988 by
Franciscan Herald Press, 1434 West 51st Street, Chicago, Illinois 60609.
All rights reserved.

Library of Congress Cataloging-in-Publication Data

Mary Francis, Mother, 1921-
   Come alive.

   1. Spiritual life—Catholic authors.   I. Title.
BX2350.2.M349 1988   248.4'82   88-11314
ISBN 0-8199-0919-X

Cover Design: William Dichtl

Acknowledgement:
COME ALIVE originally appeared in the
CORD magazine, April-December, 1970.

MADE IN THE UNITED STATES OF AMERICA

CONTENTS

Foreword	....	v
Chapter I	Life As It Is	1
Chapter II	Life Where It Is	13
Chapter III	Life When It Is	21
Chapter IV	Dead or Alive	33
Chapter V	Life Where It Is Going	43
Chapter VI	Living Convictions	55
Chapter VII	Living and Half-Living	73
Chapter VIII	Eternal Life	83

FOREWORD

This book offers an invitation. In its pages Mother Mary Francis opens the door on the bright prospect of coming alive to God.

The word in this book is: Come! It is one of the great words of God to man: Come! It was the word of Christ to those whom He touched with His presence: Come! It will always be the way to life: Come!

The invitation to come alive is perhaps the most challenging of all calls. To come alive is to take the Gospel seriously. It is to stand up to the vision of Christ. Coming alive means to take the risks of the Gospel.

In the vista of life which opens out in these reflections, the little narrow lines that are set about protected living disappear. The measured borders that define life in terms of who can run the swiftest or who can fill his barn the quickest or who can make his bank the securest yield to the arrows pointing straight ahead for the one who can love the best and give the most.

There is a clear sense of direction in these pages. Life needs direction to be true. The bold summons of the day: Live to be a hundred; Live fully; Live freely;—all these fall short because they lack direction. When a person answers the call to come alive to God, he discovers where life is.

There is another point with regard to coming alive which is answered in these pages. When one is called to come, he always wants to know how far. The words of Jesus say that we can always go farther.

The invitation which is set forth here is important to us because we have assured ourselves that we want more than anything else to be fully alive. Yet we have settled for less than that. We need to tap sources within that have never been touched. We need to open doors that have been closed.

You will want to read these chapters with an open mind and a ready heart. Don't be half alive! Never settle for a little! When you drink of the fountain of life, let the draught be deep! When you come alive to God, come all the way!

This is a book that we have needed for a long time. For it is great to COME ALIVE to God!

Father David Temple, O.F.M.

I. Life As It Is

The Divine optimism which Marc Connolly once succinctly described with as much theological precision as local color when he said that "the Lord won't admit He's licked," shines out in many a Gospel parable. While our efforts to achieve an optimistic mind on the present often converge on our building fair fantasies of the future, our Lord chose a harder but much realer attitude toward optimism: He took life as it was. And we might as well admit that life as it was when He took it up then, is essentially life as it is when some may dispiritedly toss it aside now.

An even mildly meditative reading of the narrative and prophetic parables of the New Testament will compel us with the force of objective truth to accept the astonishing fact that human life has not changed very much since the Second Person of the Trinity vested in it. After two thousand years, we dress differently, eat differently, travel differently than our forebears in human history, but we are their easily recognizable relatives. As a matter of fact, our higher education only points up the more sharply the sameness in our difference, just as our invasion of outer space and all our advanced technological enterprise only make our mishandling of earth the more painful and humiliating in its sameness to humankind's fumbling in centuries past.

However, if it was all too evidently the same kind of

humanity and the same world that Christ was dealing with when He took on human form and walked some of the world's dusty roads, His was not the same manner of living humanly with humanity in the world as ours frequently is. For He was the first great Realist, and we are more often than not very unrealistic. That is probably the reason we talk so much about realism. After all, there is no more dependable defense against the real communication of confrontation than unending talk.

There is that in all of us which seeks to evade reality. And the tendency is most pronounced in those we usually call realists, by which we really mean that they are the most unrealistic of all persons, seeking to find ultimates in contingencies, permanence in evanescence, and explanation in oblivion. Thus, we discover in eras like our own which are most passionately and even sometimes frantically dedicated to realism, a bewildering forest of defenses against the truth. All our carefully contrived myths about an earthly millennium about to dawn cannot quite deliver us from the essentiality of death's imminent night nor of the persistent night of hatred, greed, and war. Is it not because we fear the phenomenon of God which we cannot articulate that we must be glib about the phenomenon of man?

All the unrealities of a "realistic age" are spawned from a failure to seek the truth. This failure, in turn, is born of fear. For to seek the truth is already to have found something of truth. And the possession of truth is a responsibility so terrible that we are often enough unwilling to assume it. Accordingly, if we deliver our intelligence up to the unreality of accepting the world not as the convolutional path of man *in via* but as a final destination, we may commit ourselves, if we are sufficiently altruistic, to tidying up the world; but we shall fail to express the total reality of living because we have not understood the total reality of earthly life in terms of a destiny beyond the world. And, in the end, we shall not noticeably tidy up the world, either; for we shall obviously want to get the most personal satisfaction out of life so briefly given.

It is scarcely necessary to labor the point or enlarge the examples of what this kind of "earthly reality" spews on to our times, and what deviations from a fundamentally sound premise it can produce. The horizontal expression of charity which is presently so strongly accented is a valid and beautiful expression when it is seen as one arm, but only one arm, of love, and when it is understood that the other arm reaches up—to God. Horizontalism is verified only by transcendentalism, just as surely as transcendentalism is a pious personal fraud if it does not extend to fraternal horizontalism.

The first reality, then, to be established in the mind and the spirit of the really dedicated student of realism is that the earth is not our home. "We have not here a lasting city," as St. Paul mentioned some time back. (Heb 13:14) The second tenet basic to a realistic view of the human situation is that everything humanly situational has to be fundamentally situated in God. The situationally human (if you like the phrase stood on its head) is sprung from and rooted in Divine actuality. It is folly to talk of being totally involved in the world. No one can be, even if some would like to be. This is the most comprehensively unrewarding and certainly the most unintelligent of all forms of escapism. For one cannot escape out of one's Divine reality into an unenduring world. No one can be totally involved in the world simply because human involvement in earth is essentially passing and subordinate. An immortal being cannot be wholly committed to anything which ends. One can be totally involved in only one reality which is the radical Reality of God. And only in this total God-involvement can a man so understand, truly love, and appreciate the world as to spend himself lavishly upon it.

Thus, it is an easy and obvious paradox that only the person totally involved in God effects any real or lasting transformation of the world and its ills. We are, after all, most human when we accept our Divine sonship and its full responsibility. We are most realistic about serving the people *of God* when we remember that the people are God's. We need to pronounce the last two words of our now familiar and loved appellation distinctly. People *of God*. We have enthusiastic descriptions of "people-people" so needed for the cause of religion. But what is really needed is God-people. People-people have such a way of being me-people.

C.S. Lewis remarks that, "The little knots of friends who turn their backs on the World are those who really transform it."[1] This statement is so shocking primarily because it is true. And the truth has been a shocking matter from the beginning, never more strikingly so than when Christ proclaimed the Beatitudes. Surely Lewis did not intend, by saying "turned their backs on it," that the transformers were disinterested much less contemptuous of the world. Neither the indifferent nor the scornful ever achieve anything at all positive; still less do they effect a transformation. Rather it is to be understood that transformers of the world are those true realists who know the world as transient if dear, and doomed to mortality even as it houses immortal men. These are they who recognize the world as treacherous to those

---

[1] C.S. Lewis, *The Four Loves*, Fontana Books paperback edition, p. 65.

who attempt to force it to be what it cannot be—the ultimate meaning of men's lives. They have no problem understanding what our Blessed Savior meant in speaking of the world as evil and the world as good. They do not find it puzzling that Christ should send His own forth into the world, charged to labor in it and bear much fruit, and then describe His own as those whom He had called out of the world. But, if the true Christian realists have no defensive illusions against the treachery of the world, they are also the very ones who find the world most delightful, since they know it is created and contingent and passing, and they themselves not land-leasers but only pilgrims in it. St. Francis of Assisi was this kind of realist.

Francis took up life as it was in his time, others as they were when he found them, and himself as he was—created beautiful by God and damaged by sin. It is because he was humble enough to accept the responsibility for the potential good that was in him, that this insignificant-looking man who was to become one of the most significant and powerful figures in history also possessed such realistic awareness of his own potential for evil. Our urbane realism fed on sophistication and "adult" dialogue can get horribly embarrassed at that little realist from Assisi who waved aside admiration for his virtue by remarking, "I may have children yet. Do not praise me as though I were safe." The remark, however, might make good material for pondering by our more naive exponents of the new openness in intimate heterogeneous religious friendships, exponents more naive but far less realistic than Francis of Assisi.

If the beauty of his life still makes Francis, after eight centuries, God's pied-piper to captivate men and women of five continents and inspire them to fling their lives down before God in the gladdest kind of giving, it is a beauty as true as pain and betrayal and human frustration, as failure and loss and defeat. "God has chosen me to put to shame what is noble and great and powerful and fair and wise about the world, so that it may be clear that all virtue and all that is good comes from Him and not from any creature," declared St. Francis. It may be the beginning of realism in human relationships to recognize that a creature is created and creative but never creator. We ask entirely too much of a man when we ask that he be God to us. We ask too little of ourselves when we present our service of men as our sole worship of God. In both demands, we are unrealistic.

Concerning people as he found them, Francis had an all-kinds if not all-glittering variation. And he dealt with each one as each one was. Those who joined him had a single purpose and one seraphic ideal. That is, the ones who remained with him and the ones who did not break his ardent heart, did. In his united fraternity, each one was not to do his own thing but to do the one seraphic thing in a diversity of ways. It was part of Francis' genius that he could inspire men of antipodal temperaments, from the most diverse backgrounds and of the most variant views to achieve the closest fraternal unity while each remained gloriously (or ingloriously, as occasion might be) himself. Even more, while each one grew to be more gloriously himself and less ingloriously a very poor facsimile or even a caricature of God's creative work in him.

St. Francis was as realistically aware of Masseo's vanity as of Rufino's introvertedness, of Giles' sharp tongue as of Leo's curiosity. He did not wait until Masseo grew humble, Rufino outgoing, Giles sweet, and Leo detached to form his fraternity. He took them as they were and helped them to become far better than they were, in their own way, but led by him. In this he showed how truly he was Francis of the Gospel life, student of a realistic Master.

Christ's willingness to make-do with people as they are and situations as they exist manifests the Divine Realism beside which the poor little "rugged realism" of our erotic novels and pictorial violence turns in a blusteringly amateur performance. True realism is gentle, even in the beauty of its anger. It has taken men's measure and agreed to work with that size. It is when we are unrealistic enough to establish a measure to which all persons and situations must be fitted that we tend to become most aggressive about "facing the reality of life."

The false realist is often furious, frequently sensuous. The true realist is habitually forbearing, even when rightfully irate, and self-disciplined as any intelligent person who has read the score of history and of himself would be expected to be. The perfect realist is the man who is perfect in love. That splendid anger of Christ in the temple when He drove the money-changers out of His Father's house is as far removed from our violence as His gentleness is from our permissiveness. Again, His indicating "you hypocrites!" to describe those who manipulate God's law to suit their own immediate and ignoble purposes (Mt 23:13) bears no relation to the enmities we foster merely to defend the weakness of our own position and the spuriousness of our peculiar logic.

No one has ever lived as fully as Christ lived. We can dare to say that because Christ lived His own Divine-human life so fully, He was most sensitive to the lives of others—more profoundly, to life *in* others. In our case, the seeing of only a spark of life is often sufficient incitement to peevish anger. We insist on having an immediate and sustained flame. But it took only a small spark of life to rejoice the Lord who knew how to fan it persistently into an eventual flame. It was not so much that He was where the action was as that He was always where the person was. Which is to say that He was willing to make-do with the person where that man stood at that moment. This explains why His reaction to the dreariness and pettiness and embarrassment of the human condition was so different than ours frequently is. It explains why He was the optimist before the most unpromising material for sanctity, whereas we are often the fastidious pessimist. Why He was the realist, ready to take life as it is and work with it from there, whereas we are frequently the dark dreamers who belabor life as unworkable for our ideal and, therefore, to be reconstituted for our high purpose. This, of course, nicely encourages us to forget that life is sometimes reconstituted by a high purpose but never for one.

One wonders how we might have reacted to the situation St. Luke describes, when Jesus was in the home of one of the leading Pharisees (charitably unidentified) and "noticed how they (the guests) were trying to get the places of honor at table." (Luke 14:7-11) It is easy to picture the dreary little scene. Who has not witnessed or perhaps taken part in the shabby performances in which men maneuver themselves into petty positions of honor by embarrassingly dishonorable and embarrassingly manifest means? The wretched little devices employed to maintain a facade of detachment about what is so desperately wanted, the poor efforts to appear self-effacing in the very struggle for small supremacies, never really deceive the onlookers. Certainly they were evident to the penetrating gaze of the Lord. Yet, He was never embarrassed by humanity or angry with its pitiable subterfuges or discouraged by men's persevering efforts to attain some miserable little social vantage point.

It might be helpful and it would certainly be interesting

to rewrite this passage in the Gospel as it might go if we, not Jesus, had been there. Would it run like this? "And noticing how some were trying to get the places of honor at the table, the more refined persons present were thoroughly revolted. An exchange professor from Socksford was heard to mutter in distaste: 'All so bourgeois!' as he departed. And William Hennesseys determined on the spot to write a play on the pretensions of the vulgar. All the really important people present conveyed their discouraged 'What's the use?' to one another by means of their eyebrows and small, realistic sighs."

It makes, after all, not an interesting but a very boring story. The true version is so much better. "When He noticed how they chose the places of honor for themselves, He said to them: 'When any man invites you to a wedding, do not sit down in the place of honor; he may have invited some guest whose rank is greater than yours. If so, his host and yours will come and say to you, "Make room for this man"; and so you will find yourself taking, with a blush, the lowest place of all. Rather, when you are summoned, go straight to the lowest place and sit down there; so, when he who invited you comes in, he will say, "My friend, go higher than this"; and then honor shall be yours before all that sit down in your company.'" (Luke 14:7-10)

Who but the Divine Realist would be so promptly willing to make-do with these people just as they were, with their petty ambitions and their silly maneuvers? It takes either a Divine compassion *in Se* or a Divine compassion funnelled into men by grace to give the strength to make so realistic an appraisal of the human situation that you are willing to embrace it just as it is and to deal with it in the only way it can be dealt with in a given situation. If the humanest of adjectives can be applied with deepest reverence to the

Lord, one could note that Christ had an immense and amused canniness about how to deal with men as He found them.

He did not spurn talking on men's own dreary terms of dialogue—"Look! here's a safe and sure way to get a better place at table!"—if by that He could prepare men for a potent capsule course in theology: "Everyone who exalts himself shall be humbled, and he that humbles himself shall be exalted." (Luke 14:11)

Only the true realist is capable of respect for those who appear least deserving of it. And compared with the positive effort needed to achieve something true and beautiful in the most negative mentalities, outward violence, revolt, and terrorizing assume their truer proportions. It is quite arduous to be a thorough-going realist. Persistent compassion is deeply demanding and relentlessly comprehensive.

In the same way that our Divine Savior made-do with people as they were, so did He accept the life situation as He found it in A.D. 12 seq. Moneyed Pharisees, ambitious and worldly highpriests, demagogues, lascivious elders of the law and all their unsplendid company abounded in Christ's time. People ready and willing to toss a young fellow-townsman off a cliff do not seem extraordinarily lovable even when rendered faceless by the passage of time. Nor do those appear outstanding for perspicacity and insight who rubbed their chins and asked, "Isn't He just the carpenter's son?" Drab people in a drab setting were, mostly, what Christ had. (They are mostly what He has in us now, too, for that matter.) With that He worked, built, converted, and redeemed both the time and the men of His times. And in the same way St. Francis of Assisi accepted and "redeemed his time." (Eph 5:16)

For things did not look very roseate along the ecclesial

Life As It Is 11

horizon when Francis declared himself "prostrate at the feet of the Holy Roman Church." To a more cynical eye than Francis', the Church could well have appeared as Roman only in the narrowest and certainly not in the deeply indicative sense of the word. The Church's holiness did not exactly stream through many of its princes, its monks, and its religious in such a manner as to dazzle the vision of the faithful.

Avaricious prelates, cozy-living and cantankerous nuns, carnal-minded priests were sights as familiar and common as the silver-green olive trees lining the road outside Assisi. Traffic in sacred relics as well as some not just so authentically sacrosanct (one doughty pastor of souls in the Middle Ages claimed possession of the jawbone of the Holy Spirit) flourished. Dubious "devotions," the progeny of ignorance wedded to superstition, enjoyed enormous popularity. The Church certainly needed some fresh air. Reform was obviously what was called for. Things had never been so bad! Realistic Francis could not have failed to notice the situation. And he dealt with it realistically, that is to say, positively, patiently, compassionately.

Jets of scorching criticism had been hissing through the numerous crevices in the tottering ecclesial walls for a long time without producing any particular effect to blister and widen crevices. The fresh and gentle breeze of Francis was the breath of his own seraphic heart which humility had made incapable of bitterness. There had been many eloquent preachers to cry, "Reform!" by which they meant: "Tear down!" Francis understood that to form is to build, and that re-form is simply a more demanding kind of construction.

While bishops were being denounced for throwing the poor out the front doors of the episcopal palace, Francis quietly went around and knocked at the back door, which he considered in any case to be a more proper entrance for such as himself. He got in. When impassioned itinerant preachers were berating society for its sins, Francis was busy cooking supper for robbers, and sending his friars out to scout for eggs and wine for the notorious guests who were to become converts to the extent of joining his Order.

There were so many people to tell the thirteenth century Church and society how evil they were. Francis told them how good they were. He could, because he believed it. And so they were willing to listen to him when he told them how they could be better. Perhaps no one suffered more from the defections of his own, from treachery and betrayal of his ideals, from frustration, than St. Francis did. But he weathered all these because real love had cast all possibility of cynicism out of his heart. He loved as realistically as Christ, too great to be bitter, too noble to be caustic. He never took part in the work of defamation and demolition because he kept so occupied in building. His tremendous reverence for the vicar of Christ preserved him from the dubious new theologies of his time which urged instant and condescending criticism as the vehicle for expressing true filial love. And when Innocent died of the pestilence, it was sick and frail little Francis who stayed with him when the robust retinue fled in terror of contagion. This was a realism too rugged for most persons.

To take life as it is and people as they are is, in the end—and even, for that matter, in the beginning—the only way to achieve anything positive, beautiful, and good in the human situation, and actually the only way to change life or men. But it takes an utter realist to do it. It is so much easier to whine, revolt, sit down (or -in), commit murder or suicide.

II. Life Where It Is

Among the odd things that one observes about human nature, after having been obliged to observe its peculiarities at painfully close range in oneself over a number of years, is its propensity to situate itself outside the present. Our escape from the reality of the present hour takes so many different forms that about the most we can say of them is that some are even odder than others. One of the very oddest methods of de-situatedness from the present is a certain kind of immersion in the present.

We can use the present to get out of it. This may already explain the desperation with which we seek fulfillment, the kinetic energy we pour into shaking the last grain of pleasure out of the present hour. Yet true fulfillment is actually achieved by a gentle expansion of the capacity for giving, not by plunder. And one must be less aggressive toward than humbly inquiring of the present hour if one is going to enjoy it.

In the same way that we talk a great deal in order to avoid any real communication, so do we often enough become very agitated about a present situation that we must change, in order that we can be excused from growing in the present situation as it is. Some of our seemingly most ardent espousals of the present actually indicate a disavowal of the present. It is easier to shake the shoulders of the present than to look in its face. When we do, however, elect that more difficult alternative and look into the face of the present, one immediate reward is often to be given understanding that not all its problems are to be solved *instanter* so much as to be gainfully suffered in order that we may learn from them, that we may become able to turn our pathetically vast knowledge of facts and things into a gloriously small beginning of wisdom.

To achieve this beginning of wisdom and to enjoy this reward, it is necessary to forswear the company of a number of falsities which may have become very companionable if only because of their long association with our composite selfhood which, as a matter of fact, they have helped delineate.

There is, first, the all too run-of-the-mill falsity of waiting for The Occasion to do something great, while the catalystic circumstances for immediate greatness lie all around us, unnoticed and perhaps sometimes even despised. When we get out of this particular work situation, when we are relieved of the distressing company of this particular person, when our back has stopped aching, or when it has stopped raining, when people stop interrupting us, or when all these misunderstandings are cleared away, then we shall do great things for God and man. Yet, right here, strange as it may at first seem, is where the opportunity for greatness lies, the summons to peace, to happiness. For the greatness which is goodness, and the peace and the happiness, are not realized apart from God. And God is, at this hour, here. He is in this work situation which only the worker can sanctify by his presence and his love. God is speaking from the lips of this unlovable person who will remain unlovable as long as she is unloved. God is suffering with me in this backache which is the right-now and right-here means of my union with Him. God is purifying my plans with this inopportune rainfall, asking me to pay attention to what *He* asks of me in these interruptions, in these small adversities which can loom so formidably large on my horizon.

This is all simple enough. Yet, we manage to construct a whole philosophical system out of our sometimes inability to accede to this simple truth or our other times refusal to countenance it. If it is true that we must be occupied with improving the circumstances of the present insofar as in us lies, this occupation cannot be based on anything but acceptance of the present as it is. And if it is likewise true that we must move forward from the present, we may need to remind ourselves on occasion that moving forward from a situation can be very different from and sometimes even opposite to moving away from a situation. When we move forward from the present, we take the accepted present with us, both refining and expanding the wisdom and experience we have received from the present. When, however, we attempt to move out of it, we disclaim it. And that, rather obviously is escapism no matter under what alias it travels.

All of us must situate ourselves squarely in the present where a simple understanding of and sometimes even solution to the wracking problems of the present could be as obvious as disconcerting. For, in whatever of its expressions, it is love that begets understanding and provides what solutions are possible in any given problematic situation or circumstance. Love right here, right where we are. Love among men who admit that we have all made some terrible mistakes in the past and want to rectify them right here. For past blunders, past injustices, past tragedies are not undone by screaming diatribes against the past any more than by utopian songs about the future when we are all going to enjoy the terrestrial paradise we are supposedly now constructing. No, past blunders will be repaired and future betterment achieved only by loving in the present. Before we dismiss this as oversimplification, we should recall one undersized and sickly little man from Assisi, what he thought and what he accomplished.

What he thought was that love is the only really moving force in the world. He had this good thing to broadcast: this evangel, this good news indeed. And so he began, right there, right in the streets of thirteenth century Assisi, without further ado. His name was Francis, and his city is world-famous seven centuries later simply by reason of his having lived in it. Francis of Assisi was, according to Madison Avenue standards, a thoroughly unorganized person. It must be very annoying for all the nicely organized people who draw up syllabi in neat folders to see the unevadable evidence of this insignificant man's accomplishment. "Like sparks among the stubble," the Church sings in the Office of her martyrs. (Wis. 3:7-8)

That is so precisely what Francis was like. A little spark of love darting through the stubble of his times. It does not cry for proof, what even one burning spark can accomplish in acrefuls of stubble.

St. Francis loved and labored in his present. He compiled no studies on the past and made no prognostications about the future. He took men not only as *he* found them, as we have pointed out before, but *where* he found them. Francis was present to them, and so they could be present to him. And he was never agitated about where the persons or situations should have been, conserving all his marvelous energies for dealing with them right where they were. Many people said, in 1220, that the Gospel, while all very beautiful, of course, and certainly uplifting for quiet reading before retiring, had nothing in particular to do with the practical details of daily life. Francis of Assisi said it had everything to do with everything. And he proved it. People smiled, in 1220, at the idea that you could stop men killing one another with a message of love. But Francis did it.

All through the centuries, some men have tried to coerce other men into goodness of life. Negative legislation was written in the hope of achieving this. But, there has never yet been a law with power to make even one man change his heart. Only a change of attitude changes a heart. And attitudes are not altered by coercion which can effect at best only changed behavior. Even that change will doubtless be so superficial that it will only mark time to revert to the former and preferred pattern. When we change our own heart, we are fit instruments for God to use in changing other men's hearts. If we change the hearts of men, then we shall indeed transform the world. Not before. Not in any other way.

As Christ was the fabric and fibre of Francis' whole life and thought and action, Christ had to be the inspiration of the Assisian saint's determination to live life where it is, and so to help other men come alive right where they are. A ready example of the Gospel source material from which St. Francis drew what we would call his behavioral science is found in the story of the man who threw a party for the Lord, a party which we can readily believe marked at least one time in His public life when our Lord had a thoroughly good time. We know the man as St. Matthew. And if his job could be called "white collar," it could less easily be described as snow-white with equity.

Tax collectors had a bad name of which they were probably deserving enough. It was a lucrative business in more ways than by titular description. Who but the Lord would see the material for a chosen apostle sitting at the tax table, lovingly fingering the cash? If we would ever have the perspicacity to see such a potential in so unlikely a candidate, we would certainly at least want first to spruce up the material. Certainly we would want to remonstrate with him about the avarice governing his tax collecting and lecture him on the injustice of taxation in general. Give him all the current studies on the evils of capitalism to read. Send him to an institute in business administration and a workshop on the equitable distribution of wealth. Then see what we could do with him. Not so the Lord. Christ said: "Follow me!" Levi got up, and followed. (Luke 5:27) With all the precision of a Greek drama! For the swiftest response to a vocation ever recorded, there was the leanest script. But best of all, really, was the party.

If our Divine Savior took Levi from where he was, Levi-turned-Matthew did not hesitate to respond to Christ from where he was. It seems strange, when we stop to reflect, that everyone would not throw a party to celebrate being called by the Lord. At any rate, St. Matthew did think of it, right away, and did actually have a party in honor of Jesus. And because he had been chosen from where he was, the new apostle felt no diffidence about choosing the guests. You can afford to bring your real friends, unsavory reputations to the contrary notwithstanding, to eat with a Man like this. What a delight to picture that scene, that evening! The joyous excitement of all the local riff-raff (according to proper pharisaical rating) that one of their own company had been singled out by the young Rabbi who spoke as "no man had ever spoken!" (John 7:46) They would scarcely have been a subdued group. No, you can hear the laughter and the songs, the exuberant jests. It was indeed a new coming alive for Levi the tax collector, and who can say for how many others gathered around that festive board, drinking good wine and loving a good Master. We can be confident that no eyes of Levi's friends were narrow with suspicion or glinting with hope to trip the Word of God up in His speech. It is so very consoling to reflect on that evening when God had a good time with men.

It would be easy to multiply examples of how Christ spoke the "Come alive!" of His love to people right where He found them. There is that dear runt, Zacchaeus, up in his tree. The woman caught in adultery. The polygamous Samaritan who was praised by the Lord for being so clever in her manipulation of facts. Those loving eyes of Jesus were able to see in each one the wonderful potential for good that had taken a wrong turn.

It is not difficult to produce many examples of the terrible waste of the present where the non-living of the past or the non-existence of the future seem to be preferred to the teeming possibilities of the present. There are the so-called "crisis of obedience" or "crisis of authority" or "crisis in religious life." As a matter of fact, though, neither virtues, concepts, nor institutions have crises. Only people do. It is like talking about the "confused times" we live in, when what we obviously have to mean is either: 1) we who are confused by the times we live in, or: 2) we who are too confused to understand the times we live in. One who has a solemn vow of obedience, has been entrusted with some authority and has every intention, by the grace of God, of remaining in religious life unto death, and who is both delighted with and saddened by our times but not at all confused by them, may be allowed to say a word about these matters.

This is the word: Living in the present demands looking up

to God. No one can be fully human whose life is not transcendentalized. You cannot remain permanently horizontal without going to sleep. And you cannot remain permanently vertical without slipping a mental disc. Only when we look up to God do we discover the meaning and the potential of our present hour, our present situation, our present companions.

You cannot eliminate obedience by doing your thing. You can esteem and love obedience as doing God's thing. This explains why the saints have panted after obedience as the hart pants for the living waters, and why Christ became obedient unto death. Again, you cannot hope to speak with humble authority in the present if you are hoarse from denouncing the proud misuse of authority in the past. Nor can you live a fruitful religious life (or any other form of life, for that matter) while you are determinedly laying the axe to its roots. And, in the end, we must admit that seeking the Face of God quite drains us of all enthusiasm for shooting one another down.

III. Life When It Is

It is difficult to get the spatial and temporal concepts of the present separated for individual scrutiny. Much of what has been written of "life where it is" could be revolved and re-presented point by point from the viewpoint of "life when it is." Where and when are parts of each other. And although we can speak of being present in the garden, we shall also have to speak of being present at 8:30 a.m. We need not only to set ourselves squarely in life where it is, but to have an ear sensitively attuned to those highly particular and climactic moments when the ordinary obscurities of earthly living are briefly resolved and life sounds a splendid summons to meet it when it is. That is, when it is inviting us to a new response, a profounder giving, a fuller understanding of our destiny. Unfortunately, we often enough fail to hear the chimes of the present moment for meeting a need or filling a role. And, still more unfortunately, we can fail in this particularly in the spiritual life, plodding along our dull pedestrian way right past the clock that is sounding the moment of a possible new greatness.

We may need to beware of an earthbound overprudence which ceases to serve wisdom, just as overeating does not contribute to nourishment. This false prudence seems to be the commonest factor in our failures to read the time of this hour. We can be so preoccupied with the accoutrements of life that, in a real and tragic sense, we can fail to have the time of our life.

St. Francis of Assisi was always sensitive to life when it is. He answered its immediate chime with ardent enthusiasm. And certainly in his case it was no small thing to continue responding to the quarter hours of his destiny. Young and moneyed, loving and lovable, he was acclaimed "king of youth" by his Assisian peers. But then the first manifestly great moment of his life sounded. And it surely needed an acute spiritual ear to hear the chime of God's invitation to poverty and minority in that welter of wealth and ambition.

For those of us who are his followers, it is altogether too disturbing to attempt to envision what our own lives might be in the present hour had Francis not responded to the imperious summons to spiritual greatness in that hour of his. Yet, consideration of a present and completely personal freedom to fail to respond to a similar stark summons to greatness in one's own life at this hour is not less frightening but only less obtrusive on one's consciousness.

Francis must have seemed an unlikely enough prospect for the role either of individual beggar or founder of a company of mendicants. He had an obvious charism for giving, but he had yet to discover much less to explore his capacity for receiving. Right in the very heart of his singing and prodigal spending, he was invited to become listener and receiver. God merely suggested that Francis reverse his entire life's orientation, turn his whole values system upsidedown and insideout, exchange plenty for penury and popularity for contempt—and this in one fell swoop. One could envision the possibility of a young man's declining a suggestion like that. At least, one would certainly sympathize with a young man asking for a year to think it over. It only sounds like prudence. But God is not honored by the false prudence of men. And the prudence of the saints so easily passes for insanity among men.

For the saints are those who hear life chiming when it is, and reply neither: "Let me think it over" or, "Wait till I check the time with the operator." They simply reply: "Here I am, Lord! Your servant hears."

The marvelous thing about this kind of listening is that even when we do not understand what we hear we can still understand what is said. That is to say, even when we get the message wrong, we are still right because we recognize the sound of life when it is and make the best response that it is possible for us at that moment to make. Witness St. Francis again, newly "converted" to the Lord, waiting upon His Will, listening to His word. "Francis, go and rebuild My Church," the voice of God said from the crucifix before which Francis was praying," for you can see that it is falling into ruins." St. Francis listened and got the message—all wrong. And it does seem in the unfolding story of the Assisian saint's life that God went out of His way, rather, to exemplify to us poorer listeners that what is important is listening to God even though we do not quite follow what He is saying. What is important is responding to what we hear even if we have not heard correctly. God spoke of the sophisticatedly tottering spiritual edifice of the Church which Francis was to rebuild with the strength of his simple Gospel living. St. Francis understood God to mean the crumbling material edifice of the nondescript little church building he was in. And so he immediately responded to the invitation as he heard it. He started "rebuilding the church which he could see was falling into ruins."

He begged stones, hauled them, set them into the weakened walls of the little church. Even as Francis, having got the thing all wrong, was right with God for having listened and responded as best as he could, so could the prudent ones of this world be wrong with God for having got the thing right and failed to respond.

For there is another way that situation could have been dealt with. A commission could have been set up to study the situation. What was the history of the deterioration of the church? Blame the cause! Who was responsible for the state it was in? Arraign them! What policies had erred? Denounce them! Was it possible to rebuild this church? Appoint committees to explore the possibilities. Should we not build a new church instead of puttering about filling in the chinks in this old one? We know more about architecture now anyway. It never would have fallen into ruins if it had been built in a different style. Why waste time on a tottering structure? Or why, for that matter, build a new church? Let us just sit out under the sky and celebrate the end of the Church and the beginning of enlightenment. Far more entertaining in any case to exhibit these crumbling walls to witty tourists than to sweat under the effort of building. And somewhere during the protracted burden of investigating the reports of all the subcommittees and studying the findings of the area directors, the clock has stopped chiming. We have been unaware of life when it is.

Francis, straining his meager muscles to haul his stones, had heard life when it is, and had immediately replied as best he knew and understood. It was like this all his life. Even when he was wrong, he was right, because he listened to God with such intensity, responded with such immediacy.

"I'll do it—sometime" has signed the abortion permit for many a spiritual life. Someday we shall get around to listening to God when He speaks. Only, the message He had for us will already have been spoken. Someday we shall think this thing through and make a response. Only then there

Life When It Is   25

will be no need to think because there will no longer be a summons calling for response. Life is when it is. The opportunity is then. It is now.

Our Lord evinced an almost admiring affection throughout the New Testament for persons attuned to the hour. Even when they responded with highly unconventional urgency to the opportunity of the moment, He approved their alertness with miracles. There was that palsied man and his friends who were not to be deterred from drinking from the very Fountain itself of living water simply because circumstances made it inaccessible. How one would like to have heard that conversation as they planned their maneuvers! But, for that matter, it does not require much imagination to reconstruct it. "We've simply got to get to Him while He's here." "Absolutely impossible. The people are thirty-deep." "How about the back?" "Forty-deep!" "What about the roof?" "Man! A paralytic on the roof? Come on, now!" "Listen! It's now or never..." And soon, the sound of rough, eager fingers turning back the tiles, the puffing, the laborious snorts, the indignant cries from within the house, the creaking of the litter as it descended and there was made one of the most dramatic entrances ever recorded. (Mark 2:3-5)

What could anyone do with such an enterprising fellow with palsy but love him? What could Christ possibly do but heal him? But, does not everyone respond to the urgency of the hour when it concerns one's personal gain? No, not too frequently, when there is involved incurring the inevitable disapproval and indignation of the crowd, the risk of seeming a fool. Too often singular greatness is esteemed of less value than conventional mediocrity. And often enough it is judged preferable to drink from the mob's stale canteens than to step out of line and choose the living water. The hemorrhagic woman whose touching faith is recorded by Matthew 9:20-21, responded to opportunity when it was, at the price of personal humiliation. The blind man of Mark 10:46-48, heard the chime of the priceless present moment only through the rebukes of a crowd which included some members of the first hierarchy. There is a certain price to pay for living life when it is, even as concerns reaping personal reward. For the much more comprehensive rewards of personal donation, there is a yet higher price to pay.

When St. Francis hauled stones to repair the church which he thought needed rebuilding, there were those who threw pebbles at him. But, as we have observed, even when Francis was hearing imperfectly he was responding with all the adequacy then possible to him. And it was precisely this which made him an adequate responder to God's actual invitation to restore not a church building but to renew the Church's soul.

We are sometimes so encumbered with considerations of foreseeable practical difficulties that we cannot be practical about present reality. We waste so many moments of life explaining to God why His Will cannot be done, why His designs are not workable, why His invitations are ill-timed. It was, after all, perfectly obvious in the thirteenth century complex of worldliness and evil that one little man could not turn a whole social tide. If Francis' physique did not render him outstandingly qualified for the trade of stone masonry, his established prestige as a professional theologian was scarcely such as to make him the obvious choice for a leader in ecclesial and social renewal, either. However, God is not hampered in His plans by our natural limitations, but only by our failures to respond when He calls. His, "Francis, go and rebuild my Church!" to a gay-hearted young son of a cloth merchant was a newer and more radical summons in faith than Abbess Hilda's command, "Sing, Caedmon! sing!" to a swineherd. And the ensuing details of Francis' history are even more astonishing than the poetry of Caedmon.

The greatest decisions of men are made in the inner court of the soul, that same area where men's greatest wars are waged. The low voice of the Spirit of God heard in that inner court has power to lure a man out of the haven of ease into the surging waters of suffering, out of the limelight of worldly fame into the hot and blinding light of the desert, out of the comfort of routine into the unchartered dark jungles of faith. It can seem pleasanter not to listen, but in the end it is heart-breaking and life-destroying not to have listened.

Of all time-proven devices against listening to life when it is, the most effective may be the long-distance connection. Thus, it is readily possible to fail to respond to the present and pressing need at my elbow because I am so concerned about the need seen through binoculars. And it sounds so reasonable. One must not be provincial. One must have far horizons. One must not be limited by immediate concerns. It is a strange thing, though, how the history of daily experience verifies the embarrassing fact that the untended need at one's elbow never seems explained by the pouring out of the potential tender's energies on that need seen through those binoculars. An odd converse to this is that those who respond with greatest urgency to the proximate need are the same ones who, even if obscurely, even if indirectly and without fanfare, serve the distant need as well.

It is an easily penetrable paradox that one must live by an unscheduled schedule. A life is most perfectly planned whose plans are most amenable to being upset. How clearly this paradox is proclaimed in the life of Our Lady! From her earliest years, her life was carefully planned, and planned entirely for God. Apparently, just so that He might upset her plans. This greatest woman that the earth has seen became who she was by living her life when it was, when its climactic moments struck, when either its most unexpected hours or its most routine quarter hours sounded.

She planned to be a servant and was summoned to a much more arduous destiny of service as mistress of the world. She appears to have decided on obscure virginity. She was invited to inexplicable maternity. She accepted the responsibility of parenthood and was told her Child had left her because He had to attend to His Father's affairs. There could be few more consoling sentences in the Scriptures for us fumbling little creatures than that which tells us that Our Lady did not understand what He said to her. (Luke 2:50) But she listened and responded. She went back down to Nazareth to continue issuing domestic orders to this Divine Son of hers Whom she did not understand but to Whom she listened and in Whom she believed.

We are so ready to believe, once we understand. Our Lady's listening is there to teach us that unless we believe we shall never understand. Unless we hear and respond as best we presently can to the sounding of life when it is, we shall never fathom our own destiny, but be left puddling about in our shallow determination to construct our own timepiece of destiny. Opportunities to serve, to give, to solace, spring up like small flowers on our path; and we are sometimes too occupied with the business of living to be conscious of life's occurring. Yet, it is truly a fearsome thing to be too busy to be alive.

To return to St. Francis. (And what can you do, once you

have encountered that burning little man, but keep on returning to him?) He set out, alone, on one of the most grandiose programs of renewal the Church has ever witnessed, one that was to inspire rich men to give all their wealth away, celebrities to scorn their fame away, young girls to fling the shining hair of their heads away—and all these exuberant flingings as mere tokens of the joyful donation of the heart to God. For carrying out this comprehensive plan, Francis had no blueprint save his own listening heart which always heard the sound of life when it was striking. There is a kind of vastly carefree air about the whole affair.

Having heard and responded to God's invitation to change his whole life's direction, he set out with literally nothing to do literally everything. What was literally nothing? A profounder nothing than a wardrobe consisting of a tunic and a rope belt and no shoes for his feet. It was that rich nothingness of the unchartered way toward a certain goal. It was that absolute poverty of the totally dedicated listener to God, the splendid poverty of the little ones who live by the word of God and whose only covetousness is in their sweeping desire that God's desires be fulfilled. This is, after all, the heart of the real metanoia, that complete turning about, reversal of direction, cleansing of vision and heightening of hearing so that true God-orientation is removed from abstraction and rendered humanly possible. When this kind of metanoia is achieved in a man's own life, he becomes a fit instrument of renewal in society, for only then is he freed for listening to life when it is.

The gold-crusty leaf gyrating on this particular October breeze will not return to perform again its exquisite dance of death when I have found time to watch it. The old man sick and lonely today will not chime his need out to me during his burial service next week when I will have made room for him on my schedule. And God will not ask me tomorrow to achieve today's secret greatness.

Ours is an era of much bemoaning of the times. But these times are the only times we have, so we might as well live in them. Why, after all, agree to be just an automated digit in the cosmic census when one could be daily coming more alive? "Your lives must redeem the times" was St. Paul's magnificent challenge to the early Christians. (Eph 5:16) Looking at many of today's headlines, checking the plots of so many of today's motion pictures and television offerings, and scanning today's world horizon gives rather clear indication that these times could certainly do with some redeeming. But—*we*? *Our* lives? The glorious answer that is sounding right now is: yes!

It is neither in whimpering wistfulness for the past nor in neonic abstractions of tomorrow that a man comes alive to himself and in God. We do well when we sufferingly deplore the lack of peace in the world. However, we do better to recall that the basic approach to world peace is to establish and maintain an atmosphere of peace in one's own heart right now. After that, one may be fit for larger commitments to the cause of world peace, such as living in peace with one's cousins down the block, or being patient with that irritable clerk.

And so it is with all the rest. God's voice in my secret ear at this moment invites me to renew the Church and the world by my own metanoia, my own coming-alive. No one but I myself can respond to His invitation to me. Nobody else can carry out His suggestions to me. I have to live now, in whatever the situation offers. Among other considerations on this point is the consideration that to live fully in the present situation of the hour is the only way I can change what may need changing in this situation. God is in the now of my life. It is altogether a pity if I am not there with Him. When God says to me whatever is my equivalent of that word of His to St. Francis, "Go and rebuild my house," I can only respond by hauling whatever stones are at hand to put in whatever chinks I find in me and my situation today.

We accumulate some odd expressions along our earthly way. "How to deal with life." "We have to face life." Shall we, then, "deal" with life like a foeman? Like a business transaction? Shall we face life as though it were an adversary, a hazard to be hurtled? Life is not to be dealt with as though it were something outside us. It is not to be faced; it is within us. And the only way to experience it is to come alive, here and now.

IV. Dead or Alive

Among the phenomena of our times is the grimness of some of our more dedicated spreaders of joy. As we observe the set of jaw of certain apostles-of-love, we may have to confess to a fugitive inner preference for being disliked and, therefore, let alone by these folk. There comes that chilling uneasiness that one is going to be accepted in the way that a square yard of brown earth is accepted into the jaws of a metal crane. True, that bundle of earth is embraced by the crane, rescued out of the sod, and swung sky-high. But the earth, if sentient, might just have wanted to express a prejudice against being snapped between metal teeth, and a preference for lying in the sun—where it was.

Again, though every normal person wants to be accepted, to be accepted by a hurricane could be rather unsettling. Each of us longs to be loved; and if we say that we do not, then the truth is not in us. However, when we get the feeling that someone is out to love us, dead or alive, it tends to take the bloom off the thing. We are currently in danger of being accepted to the extent of being devoured, understood till we have not a corner of ourselves left to call our own. It is all, of course, only an immaturely expressed reaction against a very real wrong of the past. There is a world of good in the present upheaving of love and understanding, if only we can survive until everyone relaxes a little and allows us once more the needed human luxury of feeling sometimes misunderstood by reason of being a particular and ultimately unfathomable personal creation of God.

Is it not true that under the millennial cry of being misunderstood there is a certain satisfaction that we are, after all, quite subtle persons and not just so easily read? Neither ought we to be hotly pursued into the last outposts of our loneliness. Never to be lonely is never to discover one's actual humanity which will always be incomplete short of beatific union with God. Rather, we must be allowed a normal measure of loneliness. We need to be left a few inner attic corners where we can curl up and be unique. For that is what we are.

The love of Christ as shown throughout the Scriptures is more pervasive than invasional. He who alone understood all men perfectly, allowed men to reveal themselves to Him. For, understanding all things as He did, Jesus understood that it belongs to human dignity that it be permitted to make its own revelation. There is that hemorrhagic woman of whom we lately spoke. Our Lord certainly knew exactly who had touched the hem of His cloak and why, but He inquired, "Who touched Me?" He provided for her making her own revelation. The whole little episode is full of tenderness and humor.

Can we not hear that small, superior, and slightly exasperated sigh of Peter and his friends as they explain to the Divine Master that it is quite preposterous to be asking *who* touched Him when everyone in the county is pressing in on Him? Yet, Jesus does not say to them: "Stop talking down to Me!" or any such thing. He patiently reiterates that a particular person has touched Him, and touched His

Divine power. "I can tell that power has gone out from Me," He announces. (Luke 8:46)

So artless are his words that one waits with the Lord for an explanation of what has happened. It is not so much that He descends to the company of human limitations as that He allows us to stand beside Him and receive the revelation of a fellow being. "And the woman, finding that there was no concealment, came forward and fell at His feet and told Him before all the people of her reason for touching Him and of her sudden cure." (Luke 8:47)

How did she find that there was no concealment? Jesus had not said: "You, there! Step up and testify." This is exactly the kind of procedure among human beings that often enough readily invites concealment, and concealment at the price of humiliatingly transparent falsehoods and embarrassingly over-loud denials. People seldom so thoroughly conceal their true selves as when they are dragged into the spotlight by the aggressive understanding of grimly determined fellowship. On the other hand, it is the loving allowance for personal revelation that leaves no concealment for anyone who is still capable of a response to love.

Or again, to return to our blind man, it must have been obvious even to the most slow-witted of the multitude that what the shouting man wanted was, to see. (Luke 18:40) Yet, Jesus asked him what he wanted. The marvelous humor of God again, amid all the swirl of sound and activity, with the afflicted man crying out for attention, and the front-line marchers bristling with self-importance as they officiously bark out orders for silence. How annoying to discover that the blind beggar is so thoroughly unimpressed by their importance as only to turn up his volume all the more! Perhaps the most amazing part of it is that this officialdom-of-the-road doubtless included some of the apostles to whom Jesus had just clearly explained the reason for this journey to Jerusalem.

"They could make nothing of all this," St. Luke notes. "They could not understand what He said." (Luke 18:34) Yet, arrived only at the outskirts of Jericho, they were quite sure that they understood what was in the mind of Jesus and what was to be done. Their "Quiet, you!" to a blind beggar seeking mercy from the Master is sufficient comment on the depth of their understanding of the Master at that point in history.

And then Jesus allows the poor man to express his own need. This is an allowance we sometimes are unwilling to make, being every bit as sure as the disciples on that road to Jerusalem that we know what people's needs are and how and when the needs should or should not be filled. It is well to remember that sometimes a need is already filled by reason of our allowing it to be expressed. Who can say that the blind beggar might not have been as satisfied to remain blind if Christ had willed it so?

The Scriptures are sprinkled with endearingly human expressions of our Divine Savior's listening to what He already knew. "Jesus was surprised to hear this." "Jesus marvelled at this." "Jesus was amazed." People need to be allowed to surprise us, overwhelm us, amaze us. And while our Blessed Lord had no need to be astonished, we have a great need to have our breath taken away by other people's revelations of themselves, by other people's expressions of their needs. So often that revelation is not at all what a militant apostle had decided it must be. Frequently the expressed need is quite different from the need we are so determined to fill—a need determined by ourselves.

Besides the intrinsic human needs for self-revelation and

self-expression over which each person is supreme arbiter, there is a need to grow. Probably no age has been more enthusiastic about personal growth than our own. Our rallies, our riots, our workshops, our task forces, our protests and our multitudinously-signed representations are all calling for growth and development of the person. Only, we cannot wait.

Even though we shall all probably agree that no oak tree ever made a twenty foot jump out of an acorn in a burst of personal fulfillment, we naively assent to the popular expectation of persons doing the equivalent. We do not usually expect the child who manifests a good musical ear to write a sonata this week. For the oak to arrive, there is needed a quantity of odd-looking materials: dirt, sun, rain, snow, space, and maybe dung. There will have to be some cutting and pruning if it is going to be shapely as well as stupendous. The future sonatist will have to play many scales and many unbeautiful notes before he is able to play only beautifully right notes. He will likely get many a backache from practicing before he hears any thunderous applause at the civic auditorium.

We have to wait for the oak. We have to let the musician play some discordant notes. And we have to allow everyone a margin for error if he is to grow at all. Our Lord always did. Among other things we learn from the Scriptures, and this even without help from the exegetes, is the psychology of human behavior and growth.

What an intriguing case history on human development is compressed into ten verses of Matthew 14 where is recorded the story of a man who had faith, lost it, and rediscovered it in humility so as to proclaim it as the leader of a great communal confession. "You are indeed the Son of God!" (v. 33) St. Peter not only got his feet wet but also swallowed a good bit of salt water before he developed his faith. But, as with us all, Christ was willing to leave Peter as much margin for error as he needed.

It is such a composite of human experience, that nocturnal incident at sea. There is the anxiety of the disciples for their physical safety, followed so swiftly by their terror before a supposed ghost. It is not too difficult to suppose how we would feel in a lurching boat in the middle of the night, waves describing unwelcome canopies over our heads, and our supper churning within us. About all a seasick man might need, would be to see a figure calmly strolling down the water. Jesus' loving understanding was prompt as always to the rescue of human frailty. "Take courage! It is I. Don't be afraid." (Matthew 14:27) While the others were taking courage, Peter was, as usual, taking action.

How grand it was!—that word of faith and trust! "If it is Yourself, Lord, bid me come to You over the waters." (v. 28) Yet, for all the drama of the word, one somehow doubts that Peter really expected the Lord to go along with this idea. Maybe no man ever more quickly wanted to eat his words than Peter wanted to drink his. Still, there was nothing to do now but go through with it. And so over the side of the boat goes dear, lovable Peter.

Things went very well for a few minutes. Can we not see the marvelling disciples in the ship? Too amazed now to be frightened, they must even have forgotten to be seasick. One could be frightened about a ghostly apparition, but there was nothing ghostly about sturdy old Peter. He must surely have looked magnificent, as the wind slapped his garments against him and the waters rose and fell. And Peter walked steadily on toward the Lord on whom his gaze was fixed, to whom his arms were outstretched. But then the wind blew a bit too hard. The waters rose a little too high. His eyes looked down at the water, his arms went above his head in fright. "Lord, save me!" yelled Peter. (v. 31) That desperate human cry was not without a magnificence of its own.

And how savory is the evangelist's description of Peter's rescue! "Jesus *at once* stretched out his hand and caught hold of him." (v. 31) After all, our Lord could have let him sink and surface a few times to impress the lesson on him. Our Divine Savior did not have to stretch out His hand. More regal perhaps just to have said: "Stand!" or "Be safe!" but surely not so humanly tender as the warm flesh and bone hand of the Messiah closing around the dripping and trembling arm of Peter. "He caught hold of him." (v. 31) Who of us needs despair of our misery, weakness and blunders when we have this most precious witness that those who are contrite for blunders and preserve faith in the midst of misery and weakness, are caught hold of by God?

"Man of little faith!" the Master lovingly said to wet and shivering Peter. But he was not a man of *no* faith. He had kept faith, only not enough. How shall we ever pray and strive to strengthen our faith unless we experience how weak our faith is? Probably most men will not beg God for an increase of faith—"Lord, I believe; please help my unbelief," (Mark 9:23) until they have discovered how limited their faith is.

The Scriptural account says briskly that Christ and Peter "went on board the ship." (v. 32) The natty nautical expression is a delightful rendering for the actual situation of the God of heaven and earth climbing over the side of a little skiff and doubtless hauling a very limp Peter after him. But Jesus' love always preserved the dignity of His own in whatever circumstances. Thus, there is no discordance in the splendid finale of this most humble domestic crisis in the college of the apostles. "Indeed, you are the Son of God!" (Matthew 14:33) It was only that St. Peter had to blunder and be weak before he could be unerringly strong.

Our Blessed Lord never wanted people to dislike themselves, but only to shed their masks, unclutter and humble their hearts, and become increasingly more the marvel of his Heavenly Father's creation that each one is. It is a strange thing that, with all our pride (or perhaps because of it), we frequently will not leave to ourselves, much less to others, a margin for error. We can even come to think there is something "spiritual" about self-contempt at the vision of our failures.

Similarly, it is a common enough failing of fervent Christians to wish they were someone else. It can come as a revelation not quickly accepted by these persons that this kind of wishfulness is a correction to God. "I could be so holy if You had created me differently" is what it amounts to in the end. It is a neat enough way, too, of blaming our poor life performance on the miscasting of the Director. And it all sounds so humble. Wretch that I am! A worm among—well, glow-worms, anyhow.

Yet, we become beautiful only by an escalating acceptance of our responsibility to live in the truth. And the truth is that we do have the power, charged by grace, to come up to God's expectations. Self-hatred, on the other hand, excuses us from effort. If we agree to the image of ourselves as contemptible, we give ourselves permission to act in a contemptible way. If we accept ourselves as persons created to be beautiful and to be great, we accede to our responsibility to fulfil the Creator's purpose and design. Self-dislike allows an immediate discounting of responsibility for personal betterment.

We see in the life of St. Francis, too, all of this. The humble, unaggressive love he had for others: "Courtesy is one of the properties of the Lord...a sister of Charity, she extinguishes hatred and keeps Charity alive." (Legenda Antiqua) And these words of Francis need only to be viewed from the opposite perspective to reveal to us that charity without courtesy is dead. Charity nurtures but does not itself devour. It does not charge in, breathing fiery "joy," to carry off the objects of its zeal, dead or alive. Likewise, joy *is* contagious, but not by injection and with the victim pinned against the wall.

Again, St. Francis always allowed others to make their own revelation of themselves. Even shy Rufino learned, in the end, to speak for himself. Francis did not "draw people out" with the help of a crowbar, but listened with love to what people could presently articulate. And he ruled a wide margin for error in man's efforts to attain the height of God's hope for them, allowing them to discover and let germinate the seed of greatness within them. For this, he had to permit them a little of the loneliness essential to exiles of the earth. Truly, earth is often a lovely place to be exiled in. But no one can appreciate its loveliness who does not appreciate that he is an exile in it. The best is yet to come. And when the worst is present, it may be even more important to remember that the best is yet to come.

V. Life Where It Is Going

Even if we are striving mightily to accept life as it is, even though we have determined to live it where it is, and even when we do grow eager to catch hold of it when it is, there will still be something lacking. We will still need to have a sense of direction. Nor is there much point in allowing one another a margin for error in living and growing in love, if we have no idea or, at any rate, not much idea of the direction in which life is moving or the full height to which love is meant to grow.

Perhaps the burning question of the now long-accepted (and long-protracted) identity crisis of modern man is less a question of "Who am I?" than "Where am I going?" After all, if I have no idea or little idea of where I am tending, it might be just as well never to discover who I am.

All of us ache to understand the meaning of life. All of us strain for the security we cannot ever quite find on earth. When we do attempt to define the term of life in earthly situations, we end in frustration. What is more immediately alarming, however, and what should actually forestall ultimate frustration is the fact of initial frustration. For to set out to situate life itself in the situations of life is to begin a hopeless impossibility which will not surprisingly end in complete hopelessness. Against this there is no defense save an ever-accelerating sensationalism to beat down the interior drums of doom.

Whenever we attempt to disjoin the present from the future, the proximate from the ultimate, circumstantiality from core, we initiate disaster. There is nothing that can be explained in terms of itself alone. This prerogative is solely God's. And even this attribute, if we may call it that, of being explicable solely in terms of oneself, is God's only after our fumbling human way of speaking. For God is not explainable to us in terms of Himself. He is explicable only to Himself.

Writers on sprituality, or even spiritual writers (who can be quite a different species), have some good things to tell us about living in the present moment, about the grace of the present moment, about giving oneself wholeheartedly to the work of the present hour. It is part of our own thesis about living life when it is. But this is only part of the full splendor of truth. To live in the present moment as if it were the only moment can be either to achieve the full stature of Godlike love or to realize the full measure of orgiastic animality. To seize on the grace-opportunity of the present moment can indicate either the dedicated saint or the scheming opportunist. It all depends on your sense of direction, your idea of where you are going.

Christ has declared: "I am the way, the truth, and the life." (John 14:6) He did not say, "I am the way to life," nor did He say, "I am the truth about life." He said that He is all three, at once, without departmentalization or progression. Obviously, then, having Christ, we are to have not only real life in eternity after death, but life on the way. We are to live "in via ad vitam" since "via," too, is what He is, and not only "vita." Again, we are to find truth not just at the end of the way, but on the way. For He is "veritas in via." The thing about "truth on the way," though, is that it seems so much more painful than rewarding.

Jesus said, "You shall know the truth, and the truth will make you free." (John 8:32) Yet, often it seems that the truth constricts us, binds us, wounds us. The truth about God is so overwhelming. The truth about others appears sometimes at best disconcerting and at worst quite discouraging. The truth about ourselves seems often unbearable. So, how does the truth make us free? Better to avoid the truth by whatever means we can. Confine the transcendent God to an apartment in the inner city. Manipulate other persons and adapt them to our own ends. Establish a code of situational ethics which will safeguard us against ever meeting ourselves vis-a-vis. Supposedly once we are thus protected from the truth, we shall frolic happily along the way and find life.

Just a casual glance around the world indicates, however, that this does not seem to be working out so well. There is a noticeable lack of general frolicking. And life has been so elusive that imposing numbers of persons are taking trips out of it.

Perhaps we should release God from the constricting sort of incarnationality we have imposed on our concept of Him, stand unafraid with humble love before the real faces of real people who exist outside both our own thoughts and needs, kneel down humbly in the glory and the shame which together constitute the truth about ourselves. This is to be free. It is to rediscover the right and only way in which life is going. It is to live on the way to life. "You shall know the truth, and the truth will make you free."

What seems destructive about truth is the lack of a full acceptance of truth. It is the partial truth which fragments. The whole truth integrates. It is the half-truth which is the worst kind of lie. The full truth is shot through with splendor. Sometimes the partial truth, however, is not so much preferred as inevitable. It is bad enough to choose shadows and half-truths instead of substance and verity. It can be even worse to render ourselves incapable of receiving the fullness of truth by our consistent unpreparedness.

In the discourse at the Last Supper, our Savior said that He would "send the Spirit to complete the work of truth" in His disciples. (John 16:13) If the Holy Spirit was to complete it, then evidently it was already begun. Again, He said: "He will remind you of all the things I have taught you." (John 14:26) If they needed reminding, it is obvious that they had not assimilated and retained everything Christ had taught and they had learned. However, it is just as obvious from Jesus' words that the disciples had made efforts and used some energy. For He did not say that the Holy Spirit would begin at the beginning and redo the course, but that He would refresh their memories and deepen their insights. The Spirit would "remind" them. We can be reminded only of things we have already had in mind.

Jacques Maritain has a splendid phrase about our minds being "proportioned to reason," to what we may call "natural truth."[1] It is the oddest thing, in this existentialist-minded society of ours, how we seem consistently to reject the natural truths which press upon us with the force of daily existential findings. Experience may appear to be less effective a teacher than ever, but the actual fact is that its students are seeming less bright than ever. It is plain enough

---

[1] Jacques Maritain, *The Peasant of the Garonne*, (New York: Holt, Rinehart and Winston, 1968)

that the fragmentary truths by which we sometimes attempt to live are not bringing us good returns. When for the incessant discipline and elected austerities of the saints, we substitute an injection for "instant mysticism," what results is less the sublime folly of the saints than the ignominious folly of the shamster. A riddled psyche is something quite different from a soul shot through with the splendor of God's action upon it.

Neither does the accelerating race for pleasure seem to be chalking up any impressive figures. Three cars do not register higher on the joy list than one. Airplanes with promenades and inner staircases are not exactly jetting us into paradise. And eroticism en masse has not been able to summon that power to do and to build and to endure which a single obscure instance of pure love has always been readily able to generate. Our minds are proportioned to the natural truth of these findings. We cannot reach the proportions of supernatural truth without flexing the muscles of our minds to work with materials accessible to them.

We see in the life of St. Francis of Assisi a marvelous stretching out for truth. If he prepared himself for the remote achievement of rebuilding the spiritual edifice of the Church by seizing the immediate truth that the walls of the little church where he prayed had chinks for him to fill, he made this way of seizing the truth to which he was already proportioned a whole way of life. Francis had no blueprint for life on the day when he cast down his elegant clothes at his father's feet and set out barefoot along Assisi's roads, singing merrily enough about having a Father in heaven. He had a burning sense of direction in his life. He knew he was on the way to God. And he knew that God Himself was the way. The truth of this filled him with such exuberance for life that his enthusiasm still flames in the world seven centuries-plus after his death.

The difference between barefoot, penniless St. Francis and parasitic "knights of the road" was the sense of direction. A hobo floats with the tide, and usually with someone else's water wings to help along. Francis swam energetically. He had no set of directions, but he had a sense of direction which sent him through life like a stab of sunlight through the waters. And he discovered the truth on the way. More of the truth each day. Pondering on the truth he already possessed, Francis could be reminded of it at God's elected moments, and achieve its fullness.

God has nowhere promised that He will send the Spirit to initiate truth in us, set us on the way after the manner of packing our suitcases for us and tying an identification tag on our wrist, or that He will infuse life into lethargy. The Holy Spirit comes to complete the truth in us. He is there to "lead us back to the way" when we wander off in weakness or fear. "Rege quod est devium." (Sequence, Pentecost) He fans the embers we have struggled to keep burning and makes mighty flames of them.

The essential truth He comes to complete in us is that we are sinners called to be saints. Nowhere does the partial truth work more havoc than here. The truth about ourselves as sinners does not liberate; it enchains. The truth about God's unapproachable holiness can seem more paralyzing than liberating. But the fullness of truth: that we are sinners called to be saints, invited to enter into the holiness of God, exhilarates to the point where we can bear the responsibility which the acceptance of this truth imposes. We can see a clear example in our first pope of how partial truth constricts, whereas full truth liberates.

When St. Peter boasted how he would never deny Jesus,

even as he allowed for the possibility that the rest of the college of apostles might do so and insisted that he would go to prison and to death for Christ, he had a half-truth whose unfolding revelation was to cost him the bitterest of tears. He uttered a true prophecy of the saint who would indeed go to prison for the love of Christ and later die for Him, crucified upsidedown. He had not yet the measure of the sinner.

Again, when, after the miraculous draught of fishes, Peter asked the Lord to go away from him—"Depart from me, for I am a sinful man!" (Luke 5:8), he was wounded by the opposite half-truth. In his bleak vision of himself as sinner, the future pope had no real concept of himself as saved. After the Resurrection, though, we see Peter quiet (or at least as quiet as Peter could be) and at peace in the acceptance of the full truth which made him, at last, free.

There seems to be more in that triple interrogation of Christ than either the opportunity for confession and credo before his consecration of the first pope, or the subtlety of Divine Love allowing for a triptyched parallelism of love and denial. There seems a manifestation of the liberating power of truth. For this time Peter answers neither as the loving braggard of the Last Supper nor as the despairing disciple on the sea. Peter, the dear braggard of former days, with only a partial truth in his heart, would surely have answered Christ's question: "Simon, son of John, do you love me more than these others do?" (John 21:17) with an immediate assurance that he most certainly did, that, as a matter of fact, he loved Him more than all the others put together. On the other hand, Peter the desperate would have had to mumble: "You know I'm no good, never was and never will be. Haven't any love in me, and shouldn't be mentioned in the same sentence with those who never went around swearing and cursing about not knowing You." No, he says, quite magnificently: "You know all things. You know that I love You." (John 21:17)

St. Peter kept his sense of direction after that, even if he did occasionally wander a bit off the way. And when the Holy Spirit came on Pentecost, He came to complete the truth Peter had already worked and suffered to attain. Similarly, Christ could use St. Francis for a fit instrument in rebuilding the Church of God because Francis had first sweated to rebuild the church he knew, and as best he could. We were created without effort on our part, but we shall not be saved without personal effort.

It is altogether a pity that this precious personal effort is sometimes set at odds with salvation. This happens as soon as we stop moving. Once the search for the fullness of truth ceases, we can only either sit and stab ourselves with the points of partial truths or marry outright the lie that mortal life is all there is. That is, incidentally, one of the most piercing of phrases: mortal life. Death become adjectival to life.

Again, once we lose our sense of direction, we become realtors of earth, unable to enjoy it because we have to use it—or perhaps exploit it. As soon as we forget that we are just passing through earth on the way to the Father, we surrender truth to falsity and glad life for sour frustration. Recall the gentleman described in Luke, 12. He was rich and getting richer. His farms were flourishing. And the more promising the land looked, the more was he beguiled into mistaking it for the promised land.

One spring was outstanding. Lots of rain, but not too much. Everything greening up. Wheat doing beautifully, barley even better. No locusts came that summer, no green beetle bugs. And when harvest time came, it was a season for hallelujahs and nothing less. Actually, his barns could not hold the harvesting. Evidently it did not occur to him to give the surplus away. For he decided to pull down the barns and build super-barns. And then he lost his sense of direction. He forgot where he was headed and simply put his head in the barn doors. He stopped searching for the fullness of truth because he had the fullness of corn. As for life, he had abundant grapes and the juice of them. What more?

"Then he said, 'This is what I will do: I will pull down my barns and build bigger ones, and store all my grain and my goods in them, and I will say to my soul: My soul, you have plenty of good things laid by for many years to come; take things easy, eat, drink, have a good time.'" (Luke 12:19) He had to find out that a soul never takes its ease on earth. As soon as it ceases panting after the living water, it stops breathing altogether. He ceased panting and settled down to read his inventory.

But God said to him: "Fool! This very night the demand will be made for your soul; and this hoard of yours, whose will it be then?" (Luke 12:20)

In plenty as well as in penury, one has to maintain that sense of direction. One has to keep moving. A flabby mind is unprepared for the full revelation of truth. An earthbound man is bound to earth's stagnation. We need to be quick if we are to be fully quickened in the Spirit. We have to keep going to God if we are to discover He is the way.

"Whoever perseveres to the end, he shall be saved." (Matthew 24:13) But perseverance is dynamic, not static. It is not a matter of sitting there, but of marching on, on toward a positive goal. We can pray for "the gift of perseverance" as though it were a matter of insurance. We pay the prayer premiums and then cash the policy in at death. The very etymology of the word utters a resounding: "Oh, no!" to that brand of thinking. Persevere: to continue. That is what we need to do, continue to the end, without losing that sense of direction that St. Peter found when he let himself be liberated by the fulness of truth, that St. Francis had when he threw away worldly directives and success in favor of a burning direction of his life to God.

We shall want to do all that we can *in via* to improve the scenery. But some weeds of war and hatred and destruction and destitution are always going to remain. We do not want to be less humanly realistic than the God-Man was. St. Matthew tells us about the excited servants who were all for falling upon the be-darnelled wheat. The new wheat which they had planted for the landowner sprouted and ripened. So did the darnel. And it had been good wheat seed, the farmhands insisted. "Some enemy has done this!" (Matthew 13:28) But the farmer, while curbing their enthusiasm for a weed-out, encouraged their expectation of a wheat-in. "But he said, 'No, because when you weed out the darnel you might pull up the wheat with it. Let them both grow till the harvest; and at harvest time I shall say to the reapers: First collect the darnel and tie it in bundles to be burned, then gather the wheat into my barn.'" (v.28-30)

It is significant that he told them to keep moving. Because he forbade any frenzy over the weeds, he did not by any means tell them there was just no use trying to grow wheat with all that darnel springing up all over the place. He simply told them to keep on nurturing the wheat. He would take care of the weeds.

What a shame it is that we sometimes get this parable reversed in our lives, insisting that we have to pull out, tear down, drag out, shout down, all in the name of a good harvest for humanity and, presumably, God! Meanwhile, not much of anything is getting built. And the wheat crop is getting well uprooted. But, above all, the parable un-reversed says: Go ahead! Don't just stand there and wring your hands because there are weeds around. Keep on irrigating, God-style. He lets the rains fall upon the just and the unjust.

Our Blessed Lord's words to the cleansed leper are a glorious challenge to us: "Stand up and go on your way!" (Luke 17:19) It is the only way to come alive, be alive, and (this particularly) stay alive. Go on our way! And with the knowledge that the way is Christ, and the unfolding truth whose fullness makes us free is Christ, and the living itself is Christ. "I am the way, the truth and the life."

When St. Francis of Assisi was dying, he said: "I must hasten on to the Lord." It is what he had been doing all his life.

VI. Living Convictions

"Try to meet people half way," we are advised. Yet we say, "Hold your ground." People have a way of insisting, "We have to make compromises." But then we add: "Stand firm on your convictions." We have talked about searching for the fullness of truth. One area in which we need especially to search is that of conviction and compromise. If no one ever changes his mind or alters his convictions, we shall have rather more of a "pluralistic community" than some avant-garde writers on the theology of religious life or the "new morality," for example, are bargaining for. On the other hand, if everyone is continually changing his mind and adjusting his basic convictions, we had better cease all human relations right there. Friendship, family, community, society, religion—all presuppose intelligent stability. Or perhaps it would be more correct to talk of stability intelligently understood, by which we presuppose a hierarchical stability.

To be very blunt and unclever about it: there are things that change and things that do not change. In fact, there are things that should be continually changing, revolving like the satellites they are around the changeless verities. That kind of verity is actually not so much changeless or unchanging as unchangeable.

Once I inquired of some friends in religious life as to the

reason why they substituted such pedestrian hymns for the noble hymns of the breviary. We had just prayed one of the canonical hours, in whose assigned hymn there occurs that marvelous cry: "O God, in yourself true and unchanging, yet arranging all changes!" a cry which has shaken me anew each time I have ever given voice to it. They looked at me in candid disbelief. "Do you mean that those breviary hymns actually have any meaning for you?", wholly incredulous that they could have. "Yes," I replied, "they do." This is but a side comment not without poignancy of recall, on the second of all unchangeable verities. The first, of course, is that God is. The second, that He is unchangeable and true.

God is never going to shift His position. He is never going to play us false for the simple reason that, as mentioned when returning to sources in the last chapter: He *is* the truth. Somehow, beside the unfading grandeur of this Divine conviction, I could not fail to find hymns about all of us holding hands and being good pals together somewhat less inspiring than the breviary. In fact, it is the hymns of the breviary that seem to encourage us to hold out our hands to one another in a really meaningful and lasting way.

With all our meditating on the humanity of the God-Man, it remains difficult for us to understand practically what we acknowledge conceptually. We know that Christ was tired, but it is really rather difficult to believe it. We admit that He got hungry, but it does not seem really possible. We have Scriptural witness that He became angry at hypocrisy, angry when the sacredness of His Father's temple was violated, and this is consoling in its way but all too easily misapplied to our self-centered vexations or made the accessible "cum permissu superiorum" vehicle for demonstrations not always aimed at hypocrisy and not always upholding the transcendency of God. And there is one particular area in which we may be least able to fathom the humanity of the Son of God. It is the price He paid to be unchangeable and true. It relates to the pain He endured in living by His convictions.

We can dismiss this as a possibility neither with a sophisticated put-put nor an amused tut-tut. The most sensitive of men was the Man most sensitive not only to fatigue and to hunger but to ingratitude and disloyalty. And He did not move through His human span of years with a "who cares what they think?" attitude, but with a living sense of conviction which was highly susceptible to pain and loneliness.

Certainly there are few incidents recorded in the New Testament which are more poignantly human than the hurt Jesus was not ashamed to manifest over ingratitude. In our innocently obtuse efforts to live and to act "for God alone," we may need to remind ourselves that the Son of God hoped to be appreciated. There were ten lepers who asked to be made clean and whole. (Luke 17) Ten petitions. Evidently ten acts of genuine faith, since Christ has testified that He "could not" work many miracles in other places "because of their lack of faith." (Matthew 13:58) So, we have not just ten sufferers willing to try anything, rather in the way that someone itching madly with eczema will send in the newspaper clipping, plus twenty-five cents, that describes the cure-all, instant-ease miracle salve, more out of a wildly unreasoning desire for relief than out of any real hope or faith.

No, these ten poor rotting creatures really believed that Christ could heal them. They begged in humble faith that He would. He could. He did. And, dispatched on their way to the priests (Luke 17:14), nine of them jogged along in a predictable wild exuberance of joy. Surely our Blessed

Savior understood. We have every Scriptural support from His usual reactions to human joy and human pain to believe that Christ smiled that glorious smile which we anticipate beholding in eternity, and that very likely those warm, dark Jewish eyes filled with tears to behold the healed men's exultant dervishing. What is patently clear is that He expected the joyous bounds to subside after a few moments, the direction away from Him to be reversed, and the recovered patients to make some rebounds back to Him. He wanted to be thanked.

As He watched the nine cavorting away into the distance, and the solitary ex-leper at His feet, Jesus uttered words so poignant as to cause us to blush again at each new reading or recalling of them. "Were not ten made clean? Where are the nine?" (Luke 17:17) Thank God for the grateful stranger! How completely unbearable the incident would be if Christ had had to say: "Where are the ten of them? No one has returned to give thanks." One gets the happy feeling that this stranger did not remain a stranger, but that he became a friend who gave thanks for the rest of his life.

If Christ showed us clearly how lack of expressed appreciation hurt His human sensibilities, He did not hesitate either to reveal to us that He hoped for some human consolation in His agony. It is possible that the particular kind of horror which the objective evangelical records of the passion and death of Christ induce in us, begets also in us a kind of stunned unresponsiveness to His vibrant human expression of disappointment and frustration. The scene in the Garden of Gethsemani with the bloody sweat, the angel of the agony, the majestic: "Whom do you seek?" and "I am He;" (John 18:5) the calm mending of the servant's ear which must certainly have been lopped off with considerably less than surgical precision by frenzied Peter who was, even in the most favorable of circumstances, not the man for the operating theater—all these may cause us to fathom less profoundly than we well might, the aching human disappointment of the heart of Christ that He lacked a friend to wipe away His sweat, grip His hand, or just be there. "Could you not watch one hour with Me?" (Matthew 26:40)

And so it is with the burning convictions which He preached and by which He lived. It is such a facile, if utterly false assumption that it cost Christ nothing to be firm, that unpopularity mattered nothing at all to Him, that when those He loved turned away and walked no more with Him because He spoke too demanding a doctrine, He merely waved them a casual farewell and went about His affairs. To assume any of this would be to deny that Christ Jesus had a sacred human heart, the most delicate emotional network this earth has seen or will see, and the most vulnerable sensibilities.

If we admire St. Joseph for rising in the middle of the night to obey an angel's word that he go at once to Egypt where he knew neither the people nor the language nor the trades, we do not admire him because we think he was too phlegmatic to care about what happened anyhow, or that he was so supine that he never responded to any suggestion except with a monotonic: "Yassuh." Again, if any normal woman aches all over to recall what it had to mean to the Mother of God to fulfill the prophecies by leaving all the darling things she had prepared for the birth of her Son and to go mule-backing off to clamorous, odorous, crowded Bethlehem to bring forth the promised Emmanuel in most unfeminine surroundings, it is certainly not because we feel that Mary greeted ideas like this census-taking by a power-crazed megalomaniac in Rome by humming, "Que sera, sera!" (however it goes in Aramaic). You need not be an exegete to know that Mary cried a little on her willing way to Bethlehem. You need only be a woman. And who can doubt that Joseph set his jaw very, very firmly as he set out for Egypt. They obeyed, yes, and with utter faith and love. But often enough the heart's blood runs down faith and love. And one seems to recall a time when that Mother asked that Son, "Why did You do this to us? Your father and I have been sorrowing." (Luke 2:48)

What, then, of the Divinely perfect Son of this Immaculate Mother? There was that day He spoke to the crowd about the Eucharist. He was at the height of His popularity. He had worked a spectacular miracle to satisfy the hunger of the crowd, feeding five thousand people with five little barley loaves and two fishes which were evidently something less than the size of whales since a small boy was carrying them. (John 6:9) And a dull-eyed crowd looking for easy bread was exhilarated with the idea of making Him their king. What a kingdom that would be! Free bread. And a wizard-monarch so lovable that He could be excused for occasionally saying the oddest things. He could wither the prancing Pharisees and pseudo-erudite scribes as easily as He could cure the withered hand of a poor prone petitioner. It was His hour. But then He spoiled it all. He told them the strangest thing any man had ever said: "Unless you eat the flesh of the Son of Man and drink His blood, you shall not have life in you." (John 6:54)

What a completely tragi-comic human situation preceded this prophecy of the Eucharist to be given! We can all too effortlessly trace the patterns of our own human behavior. We have a present need. We are hungry. We are sick. We are defeated. Then someone feeds us or clothes us or rehabilitates us. And we are so entirely occupied with the pleasant sensation of feeling once more satiated, well, energetic, that we run roughshod over the fragments of goodness we ought to be cherishing. Instead of marvelling, meditating, pondering these things in our hearts, we do the equivalent of stretching, yawning, and carelessly pushing aside the fragments of love even though there be enough to fill twelve baskets of recall. One wonders which is the more striking motif of this vignetted miracle—the multiplication of the bread or the order to collect the crumbs? Power or solicitude? That kind of power is beyond us. That kind of solicitude falls within our limitations.

And then, that cry of the crowd. An exclamation which reads so magnificently out of context and so cheaply within: "This is indeed the Prophet who is to come into the world!" (John 6:14) No wonder that Jesus, "seeing that they would take Him by force and make Him king, fled away to the mountains, Himself alone." (ibid) Free lunches and "magical" performances will always be well-calculated to elicit mob acclamations of admiration as lacking in calibre as it is lusty in volume. It was not being called "king" that made Jesus flee. Was not He himself to say only a little later: "You have said it. I am a king. For this I was born. For this reason I came into the world." (John 18:37) But His convictions of kingship were removed from the crowd's as the heavens are far from the earth.

Great as was His solicitude for the human needs of men, He had come down from heaven to be king of the souls of men. And if He blithely cautioned men not to be wringing their hands about food or clothing or shelter, it was only to remind them that *if* they sought first the kingdom of God, all these things would be given to them as well. They would be as elegantly got up as lilies of the field. They would be as securely and comfortably convex as the birds of the air. The Latin verb brings to this passage a richness and delight which some traditional translations miss.

"Seek first the kingdom of God, and everything else will be tossed along after you." *Adjicientur*. Thrown along, tossed along. Here is the picture of the runner, the man sprinting after the things of God, rushing forward to give Him glory in the manner described in the last chapter about life where it is going. And the necessities of daily living being tossed to him by God!

To the conscientious objector in the back of the auditorium who rises at this point to mention that daily necessities do not seem to be tossing about very bounteously these days for a considerable number of persons, we venture to reply from a perilous rostrum that Christ spoke not just about seeing to it that all sparrows had plenty of worms and all men plenty of bread, nor about all lilies looking perfectly splendid, highlighted by the sun against the green fields, and all ladies having lame gowns, but particularly and primarily about seeking first the kingdom of God. And just about everything in world society is calculated to encourage us to seek last, if at all, the kingdom of God.

It is often a painful, searching, searing, seeking. The men who were pleasantly full of bread and fish were not sufficiently industrious even to take any initiative toward gathering up the fragments remaining from their satiety. They were apparently not notably apt disciples for seeking first the kingdom of God. A kingdom of perpetual picknicking, yes. An entertaining tour de force of multiplying fishes by twenty-five hundred and five loaves by one thousand, yes. Sensational to watch as well as tasty to consume. Such people (and who of us will dare to claim a regular place outside their ignoble company?) had a strictly zero-minus concept of the actual seeking of the kingdom of God which leads a man often enough into a desert wilderness of heart if not of place, into ridicule and earthly failure, into that sophisticatedly amused contempt which is sometimes the most galling and vinegarish of beverages a man can ever be asked to drink.

Christ knew that they were not ready to understand what kind of king He was born to be, what kind of crown and scepter would distinguish His unique coronation which these enthusiastically shouting people would largely not be there to see by reason of being in hiding behind the shutters of their houses lest they be condemned on the ground of being friends of the Son of God. And so He fled away, Himself alone. And He prayed. What did He pray to His Father in secret that night? Was it that the presently good-natured crowd might be able to bear the truth He would speak the next day? At any rate, He was not so "lost" in prayer as to forget the needs and the fears of His little band of heroes-in-embryo.

The apostles had rowed out toward Capernaum in the dark, and one of those strong winds came up again. So, there they were, teeth chattering, bailing out water, doubtless wondering why the Master had to get the urge to go off and pray at a time like this. Bad enough that He could sleep so soundly through storms that seasoned sailors like themselves considered, with all due respect to the Master's dignity and judgement, to be especially ill-chosen times for taking a nap. But at least He had been there. They could, on such an occasion with what seems to us poor sophisticates incredible familiarity, shake Him and call Him to task. "Don't You care that we are drowning?" (Mark 4) Now He was praying, literally, "God knows where." All pleasant

64　COME ALIVE

memories of the tasty fish and bread evanesced. In fact, it can be more comfortable to have an empty stomach during a storm at sea. Glum was the word for it. Where *was* He? Then, suddenly, there He was. Walking on the water again. They, frightened again. And, again, that favorite word of His: "It is I. Don't be afraid." (John 6:20)

Oh, the deliciousness of the ensuing cryptic comment of fisherman John: "They therefore desired to take Him into the boat!" (v. 21) We can just bet they did! Even the least imaginative of Scripture readers can surely see the apostles swinging their Lord and Master over the side, clustering around Him, now suddenly, casual men of the sea. They may have remarked, "Quite a wind, Rabbi"; and if they simulated a half-suppressed yawn to show how well they knew how to handle such affairs of the sea, it would never be gentle Jesus to observe that the effect of this statement was somewhat diminished by the grey-greenness of their faces and the audible nervous clacking of teeth. Christ never despised tact.

But, what has all this got to do with what we were talking about?—the living of convictions at cost of personal pain? Well, it was that next day. We remember that next day. When the crowd, in the very best of humor after yesterday's fish and bread prodigy, had rowed over to Capernaum and questioned Him with easy camaraderie: "Rabbi, when did you come here?" (v. 25) Jesus who esteemed tact, also recognized the right moments for blunt frankness. He told them that they were seeking Him with such faithful persistency because they had had a good free meal and were in line for more of the same. (v. 26) He went on to say that they should not labor for the food that perishes, which idea probably pleased most of them well enough and raised a new chorus of : "Hail, Rabbi!" But then He proceeded to say the strangest thing He had ever said. He spoke of a food that would endure into and through all eternity. And He said that this food was Himself.

There was some hedging. The people instructed the Master on the matter of their forefathers having had manna in the desert. One imagines that they did not go into detail in this explanation to Jesus that those same forefathers had made some quite plain references to preferring garlic and cucumbers back in slave-labor Egypt to this manna from heaven. And St. John was too charitable to bring in that strident note at this point of the drama. Jesus went along with them in the same meditative, gently inviting manner in which He goes along with our poor hedging when intuition warns us that God is about to ask something spectacular of our faith. "Truly I tell you, it was not Moses who gave you the bread from heaven; my Father gives you the bread from heaven, the true bread. The bread of God is that which comes down from heaven and gives life to the world." (vv. 32,33) So far, so good. "Lord, give us always this bread!" (v. 34) Somehow, though, this line overreaches itself to somersault backwards over magnificence and come down with a distinctly earthly thud. It is the "always." It is all too reminiscent of yesterday's free meal, all too enthusiastic for a very restful future. Christ's answer was that He was Himself the bread of life, that He came from the Father and to do the will of the Father. And what was the will of the Father? That anyone who believed in His Son, Himself, would have everlasting life and be raised up by that loved Son on the last day. (vv 35-40)

This was not what might be called theology for beginners. The trouble with them, as remains the trouble with us, at least on occasion, was not so much that they missed the point as that they chose to miss it. They did not say: "Would you kindly repeat that, Rabbi?" Nobody asked if He would please break down that theological capsule into its basic components. No one at all said: "We don't quite follow you. Please tell us again and help us to understand." No, with the shabby comedy so common to us all at times, they chose not a life-giving admission of ignorance but a supercilious dismissal of what they could not understand. "Isn't this Jesus?" they asked, "and don't we know His father and mother?" (v. 42) Just our own way of saying: "Who does he think he is? We knew his family from 'way back."

That He spoke the truth, a truth so sublime that only the profoundest humility could scale its heights, did not matter. He was not, after all, a "name" among those who dissected the law, but only one who integrated it with life. It all sounds so drearily presently familiar. How many dollars do we put down to hear "names" talk theological nonsense? Why cannot we listen to a carpenter if he happens to have the words of eternal life? That, of course, is the reason or at least one of the reasons why we can remain theological beginners all our lives. Or, more precisely phrased, theological ignoramuses. For, actually, to begin is already to have advanced.

Christ had no patience with this kind of thinking. Weakness, yes. Sin, yes. Fear, yes. Manipulation, no. "Stop murmuring," He said. And He repeated even more unequivocally than before: "I am the living bread that has come down from heaven. If anyone eats of this bread, he shall live forever; the bread that I will give is my flesh for the life of the world." (vv. 51, 52) More arguments from the audience. "How can this man give us His flesh to eat?" (v. 53) No more, "Master." He is not "Rabbi" now. "This man." All the easy scurrilousness of a mob disturbed by a dignity it cannot bear is in the phrase. But "this man" stands on and speaks from his convictions. He is not interested in adjusting truth to fit the situation. Truth must often be given in an evolving process. Was He not himself to say: "I have many things to tell you, but you cannot bear them now?" (John 16:12) Truth, however, can never be diluted, adjusted, or manipulated.

And so He proposed His unpopular premise from which, really, all else proceeds. "Unless you eat the flesh of the Son of Man and drink His blood, you shall not have life in you." (John 6:53) They murmured more. The agitation rippled and then churned through the crowd. "This is a hard saying. Who can listen to it?" (v. 60) And from this time, the Scriptures sadly report, "many of His disciples turned back and no longer went about with Him." The hurt, the disappointment, the terrible anti-climax to the sublime elan of that confidence: "I am the living bread from heaven!" is so achingly evident in Christ's rejoinder to Peter's affirmation of loyalty.

"Do you also wish to go away?" Christ asked the twelve. (v. 67) And that lovable old self-appointed spokesman who certainly must himself have been experiencing no small mental difficulty over what the loved Master had just said, gulped bravely and said—or maybe quavered—"Lord, to whom shall we go? You have the words of everlasting life and we have come to believe and to know that you are the Christ, the Son of God." (vv. 68-69) "This man" was still "Lord, Christ, Son of God" to poor, puzzled but persistently loyal Peter. However, Jesus' answer displays less pleasure than sadness. He answers strangely, seemingly almost not to have heard the stammering affirmation. "Have I not chosen you, the twelve, yet one of you is a devil." (vv. 70). How clearly the searing hurt of the human heart of the Son of God burns in that strange response which at face value seems almost non-sequential, but at heart value is an unbearably accurate comment on the whole incident.

Nothing could do less honor to the Son of Man than to think that standing firm on His convictions cost His human heart nothing. He showed often enough in the Scriptures that He loved to be loved. Sixteen centuries later He was to confide to an obscure cloistered nun at Paray-le-Monial that whereas He loved men so much, they loved Him precious little in return. A woman cannot help being gratified as well as shattered that such a self-revelation of God was made to a woman, Margaret Mary Alacoque by name.

Peter was paraphrasing the Old Testament, "Unless you believe, you shall not go on to understand," (Isaiah 7: 9), when he said, "We have come to believe and to know..." The current generic "we" may have to confess to getting this exactly juxtaposed. We grant that when we can understand, then we shall believe. Once we know, we shall have faith! If spiritual optometry were a branch of theology, its practitioners could do a rushing business in fitting lenses for spiritual astigmatism afflictees. We read so many words of Scripture backwards. Like St. Paul's desire to be "all things to all men." (I Corinthians 9:22) It is obvious from this fire-breathing apostle's life that he quite precisely did not mean by that: Shake hands with every heresy cruising by and pat every theological fallacy on its head with benevolent approval. Paul clearly meant that he longed to suffer with everyone who suffered, to rejoice with all who rejoiced, to be outraged with the justly irate, and to be so much all things to all as to have the courage to tell a man who was in error that he was in error. Even to tell a man who thought he had the sum of all knowledge to be known, that he didn't. Even to suggest to a man that the best place to

Living Convictions 69

be calloused is on the knees.

Our Blessed Lord could have been so much more "modern" in His approach. Why did He not explain to the crowd when He saw the shifting from acclamation to defamation: "Theology has not yet decided the meaning of what you just heard Me say." Why did He not tone down the hard saying, at least a decibel? No, He stood His ground. And if it was a hard saying He had said to the crowd, it was no less hard ground upon which He remained standing.

It was the same with the rich young man. Scripture tells us plainly that Christ loved him with a particularly tender love. "He looked upon him and loved him." (Mark 10:21) The simple words are better than any three-color illustration: the Master standing there listening to the boy's simple confession that he had done the right thing all his life, but that love was driving him to do more. Shades of St. Paul's "the love of Christ urges us." The look of love, the desire to have this innocent boy completely in the service of Divine love. But, then, the hard saying again: "Yet one thing is lacking in you: sell everything you have and give it to the poor and you shall have treasure in heaven; and come, follow Me." (ibid.) This was too much. The Gospel tells us that the young man was "struck sad" at hearing this and "went away sorrowful, for he had great possessions." (v. 23) St. Luke tells us that Jesus became sorrowful, too, when the young postulant turned away. (18:24) Yet, He stood on His convictions; and He did not adjust them to suit the boy's response.

How easy to have said: "Well, give a generous tithing of your possessions." Or, maybe, "Build one hospital to prove your good will." No, only the hurt comment: "It is easier for a camel to pass through the eye of a needle, than for a rich man to enter into the kingdom of God." (Luke 18:25) Christ said not a word about enlarging the needle's eye so that camels of imposing girth but reasonable good will and with only limited saddle packs could squeeze through. It was again a case of: that is the way it is. And we are scripturally as well as intuitively sure that it caused pain to the human heart of Christ.

Again, in the life of St. Francis of Assisi, that "Christ of Umbria" as many of his contemporaries called him, there is this kind of standing one's own ground. Francis never condemned the quality of others' grounds, but he would not be moved from his own. "Tell me not," he said tartly to some of his more broad-minded sons, "of the way of others. This is the way God has revealed to me." Which is by no means saying or even implying that Francis thought his way was the only way, but only that he knew it was his way.

The Assisian saint understood that to have an appreciative eye whose focus could share the God-given perspectives of others was a different matter from the surrendering of his own God-given perspective. He knew that one could be a sincere listener to the rhythms which other men discovered without disclaiming the rhythm of one's own convictions as they turned and evolved on a single motif. It is very interesting, in studying the life of St. Francis, to note what things made this gentlest of men impatient. Appeals, cajolery, or coercive measures to get him to change his convictions were best-calculated to raise his temperature. "Too many Friars Minor," moaned St. Francis when some of his sons wanted to adjust his ideals to fit "modern" circumstances; "I wish the world could marvel at their fewness!" He knew that most would find his sayings hard, but he did not change them. "Will you also go away?" Christ asked of those remaining at His side. He did not call after the departees.

If St. Francis of Assisi was sometimes prepared to go half of the way, it was because he was so clear about where he himself stood and because he knew what was the fifty percent or even, in some cases, the merely two percent which absolutely could not be surrendered. There is a genuine God-like quality in Francis' leadership in "arranging all changes in due season," just because he was himself so unchangeable and true.

That is, really, the point. We cannot meet people halfway unless we have taken a stand. Otherwise we are not going forth to meet but are merely wandering about. And it is not only a case of not being able to make a compromise of terms unless we have a principle of concept, but also and more so of not being equipped to compromise because we have no unshakable promise made to ourselves before God. Only the totally promised can rightly compromise.

It is so easy to confound reasonableness with unrootedness. There is nothing very remarkable about changing your mind if you have never made up your mind. It requires no great spiritual strength or psychic dexterity to alter your position if you have never really taken one. On the other hand, it is when we have subscribed our life to a conviction that we can revolve on our own axis and see a great many things quite clearly and enrichingly, remaining on axis. There is never great broad-mindedness where there is no deep-mindedness.

There has to be for each of us a life-star unchangeable and true, to follow. Only in its light can we see aright many things on the journey. There have to be in each one's life unshakable convictions for which he is willing to suffer human hurt and mortality. As Christ did. As Francis did.

VII. Living and Half-Living

When the chorus of the women of Canterbury in T.S. Eliot's *Murder in the Cathedral* beg Archbishop Thomas a Becket to return to France and not upset the mediocrity of their lives with the threat of his vibrant and demanding presence, the voices declare in a monotonous chant: "We have gone on living and half-living." They assure the archbishop that they are contented with this life performance. And they add that the greatness and glory of his presence is "a strain on the brain of the small folk."[1] They speak for us all, at one time or another.

As one writes this chapter on a Wednesday morning, it is obvious that there are two perspectives on Wednesday. One can consider it as the day that comes after Tuesday and before Thursday, and that this is what constitutes its being Wednesday. It is the day that began when we finished Tuesday. The result of getting through this Wednesday will be that we shall have achieved Thursday, by reason of endurance.

Then, there is the other perspective: that this is *a* Wednesday, unlike any other Wednesday from the Book of Genesis forward. It has an identity of its own independent of Tues-

---

[1] *Murder in the Cathedral*, T.S. Eliot, (New York: Harcourt, Brace and Company, 1936)

day or Thursday to which it is related neither by being merely prologual nor only consequent. It holds—who knows what? It is an adventure in life, a probing into life, a revelation of life. Each man stations himself at his own perspective. But to choose the view from the second perspective puts a strain, though a completely positive one, on the brain of us small folk. It demands a stretching of the soul, a reaching out of the spirit, a wide opening of the eyes, a bending of the ear, an opening of the arms. What we behold from the first perspective is very much less demanding, requiring only that we move when pushed, act when shoved, and run on a circular track when wound up by situation or cranked by circumstance. The two perspectives measure off living or half-living. And whereas the first mentioned and last described is indeed far less demanding than the other, it is likewise far less rewarding.

The thing about stretching one's soul is that it becomes consistently more expansive. When the spirit continually reaches out, it continually grows more flexible. Eyes fully open not only see the hurdles but also the way to surmount them. A cupped and bent ear hears the pleas which others can ignore, but it also catches the secret harmonic strains of nature's revelations and God's invitations. And arms must be open if they are to perform a creature's two great human acts of cradling and healing. It all requires effort. Even more, it demands decision, the decision to live or half-live.

We are doubtless fairly well agreed that we cannot personally decide to live in the sense of agreeing to be born or refusing to die at the God-appointed hour. Yet, each day we do decide the measure of our living. If we cannot refuse to die, there is a very real sense in which we can refuse to live. And it is not so much a matter of not being

Living and Half-Living 75

able to see as of electing not to see. This is evidently what our Lord meant in His description of the Last Judgement. We can stop at the facile denouncement of the people who never grasped the living presence of Christ in His members. "Lord, when did we see You hungry and did not feed You? When did we see You thirsty and not give You anything to drink?" (Matthew 25: 31-46) We know the rest of that wounded litany of counter-reproaches to the Lord. But there is a far profounder denouncement which the Lord evidently purports to make in this Gospel narrative: the judgement on those who did apprehend the living Christ in His members but did not accept the consequences.

Honest Saul on the road to Damascus was definitely not half-living. He had business to execute. And that is an unintended facile pun on his business which was precisely to execute—Christians. That these people had a radically vital connection with Christ, and that Christ was God, were the matters which Saul had to be struck blind in order to see. When he saw, he did not look away. He never pretended not to see, even when physically he could not see. He never settled for half-living. Executor or executed (as he was eventually to be), this man lived his life in full measure.

But what is the connection between our considerations of Wednesday, the Last Judgement, and Saul on the road to Damascus? Actually, a very close one.

The person who enters into Wednesday with a sense of high adventure will never find only drabness in the drabbest of Wednesday situations. For, as a matter of fact, it is half-living that creates drabness. Yet, there is that in all of us that leans toward half-living and fears the strain on the brain which whole living exerts. Each one's summons to personal greatness is an invitation so eminently personal that no one in this world save that particular person can respond to it. That this greatness is achieved more by receptivity than by activity as such is the mystery of Wednesday and of life. This alertness to life is not less particularly and happily noticeable in St. Francis of Assisi than in St. Paul.

Francis never attempted to sketch out nor did he desire a blueprint of life. To him it was an unfolding mystery, and his greatness on which history has so enthusiastically commented and which his posterity has so largely monumented lay in his openness to life's unspooling direction. Just as the turned-in movement of a dancer calls down the wrath of the ballet-master and the turned-out movement of the authentic danseur elicits the viewer's delight in its fresh revelation of the grace and beauty of the human body, so does a turned-in life testify to dispiritedness while an opened-out living gives witness to exultation of spirit.

The thing is, we never know. Never know what purifying sorrow or enlivening joy awaits at the turn of the road. We have to watch, if we are to see. We have to walk with eagerness to the turn of the road if we are really to arrive, and not just get there. We have to hold out the arms of our spirit with a full sense of wonder if we are to gather in the mysteries of today which will reveal us to ourselves. It is only in the willingness to accept the revelation of life in other people that we are revealed to ourselves. It is only in the openness to the revelation of the moment that the totality of life can be increasingly revealed to us.

Thus it was that the poor women of Canterbury would not bring themselves to accept the revelation of life in their archbishop. Because he stood firm against domineering kings and flabby-souled prelates, because he was willing, and this not without the martyrdom of the heart, to accept the challenge to greatness in his own life, the women and their company feared to remain in his presence; or, more precisely, to allow him to remain in theirs.

For greatness is contagious. And the women were rebelling against greatness. It is a strange thing, this rebelliousness that lurks in us all. What we admire in our heroes we fear in ourselves. And the fear can be camouflaged in many ways, the very worst of which is the righteousness which calls itself fidelity. So can a "faithful wife" spend a whole lifetime of half-living. Meals are cooked, socks are mended, the house is cleaned. She surrenders her person to her husband and bears his children. She prepares his favorite dishes which she herself does not like, and goes to the plays that interest him when they bore her, all of this with a satisfying sense of personal holocaust. All these and a thousand other praise-worthy-things-in-a-woman she can do without ever rising to the greatness of love. What is it, then, this greatness?

Greatness of love, wholeness of living, is the increasing penetration of the mystery of love and of life. It is the all-demanding, all-pervasive, all-inclusive openness to life as God increasingly reveals to us its mystery in Himself and in others. And the lack of this greatness? Oddly enough, not just either set-jawed dutifulness or slack-armed apathy, but, most subtly of all, comfortable "fidelity."

We just mentioned the pseudo-faithful wife who never achieves the greatness of life, of love, or of herself. It is the same for the husband. It is the same for the nun or the priest. It is not enough for the husband to be the provider, the sovereign, the lover, the father, in order to escape the half-living of his life.

It is not enough for the nun to be submissive, observant, punctual, pleasant, compliant. Praiseworthy all of these things, but possible in half-living and not at all necessarily productive of whole living.

One has to be always waiting to be used, always ready to be given, always wholeheartedly, wholespiritedly and wholemindedly alert to the glorious danger of greatness. Whether it be a question of religious love, marital love, filial love, apostolic love, the two possibilities remain: living or half-living. If we are not ready to die for what and whom we love, we have never wholly lived. And this kind of dying is not the release from life, but the penetration of life. This can be either to go on living or, literally, to die.

Just as the scrubbers and sweepers of Canterbury wished to keep an ocean between them and their loved archbishop lest he draw them into the terrifying vortex of his own greatness, lest they be forced to take a stand, so can we pile up sandbags of the currently popular "confusion" against the necessity of standing forth on our convictions. It is not only easy but presently also fashionable to be "confused." One escapes criticism and takes in sympathy. These same dubious comforts and sympathies are often enough an acceptable portion to the apathetic and unreceptive and all those who rebel against their vocation to greatness by half-living.

God has used some quite forthright language in describing His personal reaction to the listless, the apathetic, the half-livers. "I will vomit them out of my mouth." (Revelation 3:16) God not only explains that He is enthusiastic about saints, but issues a hopeful prognosis for energetic sinners when He says: "Would that you were either hot or cold." (ibid.,15) But He describes His feelings about the lethargic, the closed-in, the foot-draggers in that expression which is neither as sophisticated nor as urbane as an acceptable drawing-room-type God should employ. What sort of peasant-tongued God is this who says: "But because you are neither hot nor cold, but lukewarm, I will begin to vomit you out of my mouth?'' ''Now, really, God!'' is what we may embarrassedly comment.

Why does God scorn the drearily cautious, the electively blind, the selective sinners who exercise iniquity only in socially acceptable ways and decline to make the effort necessary to be either great saints or great sinners—which is the label of that portion of potentially great saints who directed their splendid energies down the wrong road? Is it not because God cannot be comfortably blissful that His magnificent gift of life is being carefully budgeted whereas He intended that it should be lavishly spent? There is a very revealing event in the early life of St. Francis of Assisi quite to this point.

Young Francis had gone on pilgrimage to the tombs of the apostles in Rome. He stood by the tomb of St. Peter and watched the wealthy pilgrims putting down their all-too-carefully measured (our income tax-deductible) offerings before the prince of the apostles. With that splendid scorn of his, Francis grabbed hold of his own pilgrim's wallet and turned it inside out, the gold coins spinning crazily along, bright as joy in the Roman sunlight. The incident is his own peculiar kind of prudence. For, whereas other men might have taken thought for putting enough aside for noonday spaghetti, and whereas other pilgrims might have considered the budgetings indicated for a comfortable return journey, St. Francis lived the moment completely, finding the total and immediate giving more satisfying than spaghetti and the absolute spendthriftery more comforting than cushions.

All his life long this was Francis' *modus vivendi:* a whole living, a whole giving, a whole openness to what offered at the moment. And although forty-four years of earthly life might seem a short span in some men's calculations, it was long for Francis because it was the complete span of a fully-lived life. We could put it this way: that all his life long, short as it was, exuberant Francis lived. He appreciated in full measure both water and wine, both fasting and the almond cookies which he accepted in his dying hours along with fiddling. He was never a self-conscious "saint." He loved and he lived to the full of it. He founded a great Order and he made human blunders. He was capable of ecstasy and of vexation. He blessed some of his sons and he cursed others who, as he said, pulled down what he and the others built up. And his was never the inglorious achievement of not having blundered because of not having assayed. Francis could have been as great a sinner as he was great a saint, but he could not have been a halfway sinner or a maybe saint. Half-living was not for him. He was not afraid to be great. God's summons to a totality of living put no strain on the brain of this small man from Assisi.

It is not sorrows which deplete us so much as sorrows half-accepted. The Cross is salvific only when it is carried, not when it is grudgingly dragged along.

But, to return to Wednesday: I am not going to be the same Wednesday evening as I am this Wednesday morning. Whether I shall be more shrunken or more expanded in spirit, more impervious or more alert to life on Thursday depends on how I live Wednesday. A wife who truly loves will have more insight into her husband at the end of this day than she had at this day's beginning, just as the nun who is humble enough to reconcile a call to the greatness of whole-living for God with the deficiencies of a nature addicted to half-living since the Garden of Eden was first "closed for the duration" will have more insight into Christ at this day's end. It can seem so unimportant not to respond to the subtleties of love which God proposes. A normal person feels at least somewhat ashamed of his roaring impatience. In fact, it may even take him three cigarettes to rationalize it to himself. But just not to be patient is so socially acceptable that one can comfortably live with it. To put it succinctly: it normally hurts us to witness our smallness, whereas it is often not particularly painful at all to espouse our non-greatness.

This is what we have been trying to say about Wednesday. Once we have traded Wednesday's possibilities of sanctity for either robot-like dutifulness or petulant performance, it is so much easier to be a robot or a peeve on Thursday. God sounds the call to greatness in every human heart. Yet to every human belongs the possibility of turning down the volume or even dialing out.

St. Francis of Assisi was always answering that summons to greatness, and so it grew ever more imperious in his ears, leading him from easy riches to penury, from popularity to contempt, from such surpassing rewards as the approval of the neighbors to the crucifying approval of God even unto the stigmata engraved upon his worn-out little body.

Then there is St. Paul whom we left sitting on the road to Damascus several pages back. He heard the call to greatness, too, as he sat, blind, on that dusty road, and resolved to give up his favorite hobby of killing Christians in favor of being himself beaten and shipwrecked, flogged and derided, and finally beheaded. Francis did not hear God's voice in his heart saying: "Go and rebuild my Church which is falling into ruins," and chase back to the city to confide to his comrades that one gets the oddest ideas in damp churches in the evening. Nor did Paul get up on the road to Damascus, shake the dust from his tunic, and tell his fellow-riders: "I should never have been riding bareheaded in this strong sunlight. A man starts thinking he's hearing things." Neither did he put the first century equivalent of sun-glasses on his Sun-blinded eyes and gallop on to the Christian-hunt. Both men listened and agreed to accept the call to greatness. Half-living ended for Francis in a tumbledown church, for Paul on a dusty road. It need not end quite so dramatically for us. But it had better end.

Where, then, is the end for us? Surely not when we join the indignant line of the old, old chorus, droning: "Lord, when did we see You hungry and did not feed You? When were You in prison and we did not visit You? When were You naked and we did not clothe You?" (Matthew 25:31-46) Satiety is most destructive by way of its destroying healthy hunger. There are lonely prisons of the spirit where visitors fear to come. And there is a nakedness of the stricken heart too terrible for any but the great of heart to sear their eyes with seeing. That may be part of the parable.

It was when the frightened sweepers of Canterbury allowed themselves to be drawn into the vortex of their archbishop's greatness that they became great. It was when they agreed to throw in their humble lot with his inevitable martyrdom that their lot became enduringly great. And so, when they stopped rebelling against greatness and the wholeness of living their lives, they said with all truth of contrition: "Forgive us, Thomas, Archbishop!"

Forgive us, God, Lord Jesus Christ! Redeem us from half-living into living.

VIII. Eternal Life

One is given life in order to spend it. And that seems so self-evident that one wonders why we often manage to get it counterposed so that it reads: one is given life in order to save it.

Yet, a compassionate Christ knew that there is that in all of us, or at least in most of us, that makes us want to hold on to earthly life. It is, after all, our only complete personal possession, even though we were not consulted about its being given, have not been polled about the hour most suitable for its ending, and sometimes seem at least circumstantially and situationally to have little to say about its unfolding. It is beneath the surface of circumstances and far beyond the merely situational that we are each of us leasers on life between its rational starting point and its terminus.

What we expect of life, how much and what, are each one's extremely personal decisions to make. Unless, of course, one opts for the herd mentality which is a kind of decision although more automated than expressive of individuality. Again, whether he saves up his life and in what amount and in what safety deposit vaults or (even worse) in what savings account drawing selfish interest on his own life, is likewise each man's business to decide. Hence the counsel of Christ; if you try to save your life, you will go bankrupt; whereas if you fling your life away in love, serving Him and His people, you will get a very curious return: you have saved your life and become rich forever. He will save his life. "Anyone who loses his life for my sake will find it." (Matthew 10: 39)

Actually it should not be too surprising that the Lord who always showed more inclination toward the ardent, the spendthrift, the generous, than toward the cautious, the calculating and the sparing, should offer such climactic counsel about life in general. It was after all, His own Divine-human *modus vivendi*. Christ was Manalive beyond what the hero of Chesterton's novel of that same name could hope to be, since Christ was the perfect Man and therefore capable of fullest living. And it is the Christ of the Gospels who is always turning before our eyes the many-faceted diamond of the truth which He taught and which He also is. The paradoxes of that truth are His continuing evangel to each of us in our individual lives.

One will be ready to live life as it is now, in the circumstances that are and the situation that presently prevails, only if one is coming daily better to understand that it is only in eternal life that terrestrial life will be made wholly explicable. Again, one becomes clear about the road maps of earthly life only after having realized that the itinerary does not end on earth.

Or, when is life? Now and forever—as the Church has rounded off her prayer from forever and does now. Often enough the "now" is simply humanly unacceptable without the "forever." "Eye has not seen, nor has ear heard, nor has it entered into the heart of man what things God has prepared for those who love Him." (I Corinthians 2: 9) Just the pondering of that scriptural statement is itself a raising of us to life from all our dyings. For, if we love God, then one day our eyes will see clearly, our ears will hear plainly, and into our hearts will enter the joy of eternal life.

The person alive lives with a sense of direction, has convictions about the road to be travelled, and renounces the option of living and half-living in favor of that total vitality with which St. Francis of Assisi and all those "holy men and women saints of God" sped, staggered, stumbled, and struggled into eternal life. They did not arrive at the eternal gates as camels too well-bagged to pass through that Deific eye of that celestial needle. Rather, they had spent all of earthly life on living it. Now, free and unencumbered, they set upon spending eternal life in living it.

"Holy! Holy! Holy!" they cry out before the throne of God in eternity. It is so good to have long practiced those lyrics of that eternal song on earth and thus, even here below, to have truly come alive.